LARRY PUESCHEL

Blue Ghost

A helicopter pilot writes home from 1968 Vietnam.
"Don't worry about me. Us Gun–Pilots are invincible!"

To Gloria (Lafond) Pueschel, teacher, mother, grandmother, sister, friend, and a great person who is missed by many.

To the soldiers who fought in the Vietnam War. It was a tough war and you were part of it.

To the veterans and soldiers from all wars, especially those who wrote home from wherever they were to whomever they wrote.

A special Thank You to all the men and women in the armed forces for their service.

"During the day on Monday, Washington time, the airport at Saigon came under persistent rocket as well as artillery fire and was effectively closed. The military situation in the area deteriorated rapidly. I therefore ordered the evacuation of all American personnel remaining in South Vietnam."

— President Gerald Ford, April 29, 1975

Contents

Preface

My brother Tom, we kids called him Tommy, was four years older than me. I looked up to him in about everything. He was the firstborn in our family, so maybe that made him seem even bigger in life to me and my brothers and sister. He set a path that was a good path for anyone who tried to follow.

I always thought he was really cool, way cooler than me, kind of out of my league. He wasn't big, kinda thin—too thin, Mom would say—at 5' 11' and barely 150 pounds, she could make her case. He had thick brown hair, and clear blue eyes that spoke of a good heart. He wore his sunglasses in a really cool way. Tom loved music and the arts; he could play both guitar and piano and sing and dance with the best of them. And draw—boy, could he draw. He painted beautiful pictures and some odd ones, too. He loved to read and had a fondness for poetry. Important to me at the time, he courted the ladies with an easy charm and a quick smile, while I was mostly afraid to speak to them. He talked easily to people, and people responded to him and loved him.

He always seemed happy. His best friends came over to laugh and talk, play records from Tommy's 45 RPM collection, as they got ready to go out on the town. I invaded his record collection from time to time, as did my siblings. He mostly let us, if we were careful and put things back...with no scratches, please. When my friends came over to the house, the first thing

I wanted to do was have them meet my brother, or at least see him, and he was kind of accommodating, if only for an instant. He was impressive in many ways, even in his teenage years. And I loved him dearly. And always will.

Then the Vietnam War happened...

All America could see the tragedy that was the Vietnam War. We had front-row seats as we watched events unfold every freaking day from our TV sets. We saw and heard the gunfire, the tracers and the bullets and the rockets and the mortars, and we saw the troops patrolling the streets, walking the highlands, and hacking through the jungles. We saw the helicopters, flying around like geese in formation, one after another, all lined up. Helicopters were used for everything – transporting troops, medevacking the wounded, scouting and signaling where the friendlies were and where the enemy was, and most deadly of all, attacking. They were employed in command-and-control and, of course, for flying a general or two around. To accomplish these things, the helicopters were in great danger—taking fire while giving fire back, all the while hovering like a sitting duck. They had to fly low and be in and out quick. It was no easy job.

From our TV sets, we watched and listened to the war correspondents telling the story-of-the-day. We heard Walter Cronkite, in his deep, solemn voice, and his forlorn looking face, report the war news to us on a nightly basis. We saw the wounded, could almost feel their pain, and we stared at the blood right in front of our eyes. Though our TV sets were black and white, we knew it was blood, no doubt about it. And then there were the body bags, being transported back home, telling us of the toll the war was taking on our troops. We cringed thinking of the lost lives and wondered why. We could only guess at the pain many American families endured at the loss of a loved one. We hoped and prayed and thought that it would never happen to us or our family or a family close to us. But it did. It was a war that affected most of us on the home front, and we agonized over it.This horror of war visited us on a daily basis, droning into our minds and hearts. We didn't understand why we were there, why this was going on, and what was happening to us and to our country. The Government didn't help much either, but they sure cooked up almost believable rationales.

Vietnam was ugly and brutal, and most of all, very sad. The year 1968 was the bloodiest and most deadly year of the war.Troop levels were at their highest (536,100 American troops) and the fighting was at its worst. Warrant Officer Thomas R. Pueschel was in the middle of it all.

During his time in Vietnam, from October 1967 through December 1968, he served with Troop C, 7th Squadron, 17th Air Cavalry (67-68) which was later re-designated as F Troop 8th Cavalry (68). They were known as the *Blue Ghosts* or *"Ma Xanh"* in Vietnamese. For most of his tour in Vietnam, Tom was stationed at Chu Lai Air Base, on the south-central coast of Vietnam, just miles from the battlegrounds of Dak To, Quang Tin, Tam Ky, Kham Duc, Quang Ngai, and DaNang. The *Blue Ghosts* would be out there, in the forefront, in every one of these fights.

Thomas R. Pueschel 1967

He would serve 423 days in total, about 13½ months. He would say in his later letters, *"It's been such a long, long, long time since I left last October — a terribly long time…"* Tom had left his good, happy, fun-loving life at home to come face-to-face with the tragedy of the Vietnam War. He left his close family and his friends behind. He left his girlfriend behind, too, after they became engaged to be married, just before his departure. It wasn't all bad for him. The Army helped him realize his boyhood dream of flying, and he was, at times, happiest being *"up there singing love songs to the sky."* He loved flying his helicopters. Only problem was, he was flying them in the middle of a war, and they had guns on them.

Tom flew his UH-1C Huey gunship, and later the Cobra AH-1G fighting helicopter, in over 900 aerial combat missions over hostile territory. He saw many a bullet and he sent out many a bullet.

Much of Tom's story is told in his own words, through the many letters he wrote home, revealing his changing thoughts and insights. He attempted to call out for some of the normalcy of life he left at home. He wrote of his loneliness and a feeling of helplessness. And then there was his utter joy of flying that crept onto the pages!

The story is also told by those close to him—his family, friends, and the soldiers who lived and served with him. It's a story of the times, the decisions made by others that Tom and his fellow soldiers had no control over or say in but greatly affected their lives. It's also a story of the turmoil on the streets at home, the confusing politics behind the war, and the overall craziness of the world around him.

This is but one story of the many stories of the Vietnam War and the many soldiers who did their job, followed orders, and answered the call of duty. They knew what they had to do, and they did it with great courage, extreme valor, and true honor. It's part of the history of the many brave men of those times.

This is the story of his 423 days in Vietnam, or at least, part of the story...

Acknowledgement

My thanks to Gloria Pueschel, for providing documents and pictures in a shoe box, and to her two sons, Mike and Josh. Also, to Tom's parents, Richard and Erna Pueschel, for enduring 1968 and for faithfully saving the great majority of Tom's letters home.

My gratitude to John Shephardson for his first-hand knowledge and perspective, for his quotes and comments, and for providing various supporting materials including the Greg Ross video. John was in a sense the technical advisor. He was there. He saw it firsthand. His insights were truly invaluable.

To the many relatives and friends who provided their support and encouragement while I was producing this narrative. Also, to Tom's friends, Bill Utley and John Zokowski, for their stories and insights.

The internet and its seemingly infinite sources of data, stories, and reference materials that included several Blue Ghost members' sites.

The public libraries of America where there are a multitude of stories and facts about the Vietnam War, all of which should not be forgotten.

And I would also thank Gail Pueschel, for reading and listening and providing her insightful and valuable feedback.

I'm in the Army Now!

It was 24 November 1965 when it came in the mail. The envelope that it came in was in itself ominous. For most every young person at the time, it was a letter that they didn't want to get.He could see that the return address in the upper left-hand corner of the envelope which read "Selective Service, Local Board No. 75, Hampden County, Room 205 U.S. Post Office, Holyoke, Mass. 01042." The letter was addressed to Mr. Thomas R. Pueschel. As he opened the letter, its words jumped out directly at him, "You are hereby directed to present yourself for Armed Forces Physical Examination to the Local Board named above by reporting at: Local Board #75, Post Office Building, Holyoke, Mass. On 6 December 1965 at 6:30 AM."

And so, Tom's trek into the United States Army began. The actual physical turned out to be in neighboring Springfield, where Tom and his cousin Bob went together on the 6th of December 1965. That day there were nearly twenty boys all lined up readying to take their physicals. It was a cold winter day, and the building was drafty and the boys plenty nervous. The physical itself was divided up into four different stations with four different doctors, each administering different types of physical tests. Tom and Bob took their turns at each station

1

and met outside afterwards. Tom looked at Bob and Bob looked at Tom, as if to say to each other, "Well, how'd you do?" Bob had made it through the first three doctors' stations, but Bob's asthmatic medical condition identified in the final station precluded him from passing the physical. Bob was not happy. He had so wanted to pass but it wasn't to be. Tom looked at Bob, and plainly said, "Looks like I'm going into the Army."

Tom enlisted in the U.S. Army on 21 February 1966. He headed to basic training the next day and arrived at the U.S. Army Reception Station in Fort Polk, Louisiana. Basic training had begun. It would be eight weeks of learning how to be a soldier: from marching to firing weapons, from proper hygiene to treatment of wounds, and most importantly, taking orders from superiors.

Tom had signed up for the Warrant Officer Training Program which was the basic program for training U.S. army soldiers to be helicopter pilots, with the majority of graduates heading to Vietnam. The program had two phases – the first or primary phase began on 14 May 1966 at the Army Primary Helicopter School in **Fort Wolters-Texas (66-23)** and lasted 24 weeks. Training was learning the essential elements of flight — hovering, auto-rotation, navigation, and night flying. It also included a heavy classroom study of weather and systems. Half day in class, half day flying.

The second phase was at the Army Aviation School in **Fort Rucker-Alabama (67-1)**, which began on 1 November 1966 and lasted 19 weeks. At Fort Rucker, the training was focused on the transition to Huey helicopter, instrument flight, tactical training, and firing aircraft weapon systems. Upon graduation on 14 March 1967, Tom was appointed as a Warrant Officer and received his wings.

Tom and his helicopter, Fort Wolters, TX (left); Getting his wings, Fort Rucker, AL (right)

On 20 April 1967, his unit headed to the **Fort Knox-Kentucky U.S. Army Armor Center (USAARMC)** which was the final leg of their training. The training would last 24 weeks with primary emphasis on learning to function as a unit, learning all aspects including scouts, guns, lift, and infantry. All soldiers had to write their "Last Will and Testament" and have body identification pictures taken. Tom finished his training at Fort Knox on 6 October 1967 and punched his ticket for a 12-month tour in Vietnam, which would start in just four days on 10 October 1967.

Getting your "Personal Affairs" ready

"When completing this booklet, remember that it represents your instructions to your beneficiary in the event of your death...." So began the 15-page Disposition Form 2496-1, Subject: Personal Affairs" booklet that each soldier was required to fill out. The booklet was to be prepared in the event of death and included a Will, Power-of-Attorney, Death Benefits information, references to insurance documents, other personal and financial items.

Tom Pueschel wrestled with the form, hardly completing many of the items on the "Personal Affairs Check List". He sat there biding his time, doodling and drawing on the top page of the disposition form and then inscribed this poem on the front of his booklet:

These, in the days when heaven was falling,
The hour when earth's foundations fled,
Followed their mercenary calling
And took their wages and are dead.

Their shoulders held the sky suspended;
They stood, and the earth's foundations stay;
What God abandoned, these defended,
And saved the sum of things for pay.

This poem entitled "Epitaph on an Army of Mercenaries" was written by A.E. Housman, in which he honors the bravery of soldiers in the face of great odds. It was written during the early stage of World War I to honor the British soldiers and mercenaries who fought with valor at the battles of Ypres. ... .For Tom, he knew where he was going — to the ugly unfriendly skies of Vietnam and could only think about about his chances of surviving and coming home. He was worried.

DISPOSITION FORM (AR 340-15)

T.R. PUESCHEL
W 3155673

REFERENCE OR OFFICE SYMBOL	SUBJECT
AJRTB-WO2	Personal Affairs

TO All Personnel   FROM CO, 2d WO Cand Co   DATE 21 Sep 66   CMT 1

1. The attached document has been assembled to assist you and your dependents in keeping up with your personal affairs. If you use the information and sample sheets properly, it will become the most valuable document you possess.

2. I urge you to take the time to read over the packet, comply with the instructions, fill in the appropriate information and then put it in a safe place with the rest of your important papers. If you are married your wife should have this document when you go overseas. In the event you are single, you should leave the document with your next of kin.

3. I hope you will find this packet helpful in organizing your personal affairs.

1 Incl
as

William E Tower
WILLIAM E TOWER
Captain, Infantry
Commanding

"... THESE IN THE DAY WHEN HEAVEN WAS FALLING,
THE TIME WHEN EARTH'S FOUNDATIONS FLED,
FOLLOWED THEIR MERCENARY CALLING,
AND TOOK THEIR WAGES AND ARE DEAD.

THEIR SHOULDERS HELD THE SKY SUSPENDED,
THEY STOOD, AND EARTH'S FOUNDATIONS STAY,
WHAT GOD ABANDONED, THESE DEFENDED,
AND SAVED THE SUM OF THINGS FOR PAY..."

Disposition Form 2496-1, page 1; Housman poem and Tom's drawings in blue ink

* * *

Letter sent home from Fort Polk, Louisiana, 23 February 1966, two days after arriving for basic training.

23 February 1966

  Dear Mom & Dad,

  I finally got some free time, so I thought I would drop you a few lines to let you know how things are down here. First of all, I came down to Fort Polk with two other guys from Springfield who are also in the Warrant Officer Training Program. They are both in the same class with me, #66-23. We took four planes getting down here — one from Bradley Field to Newark, N.J. There we changed planes and went to Atlanta, Georgia. From Atlanta, we took another plane to New Orleans. From New Orleans, our fourth plane went to Lake Charles, LA. From Lake Charles, we had to take a bus to Leesville, LA, which is right outside Fort Polk. One thing I can't understand is that we are so far south, and yet you wouldn't know it from how cold the weather has been. If I didn't know better, I'd say this was New England. I hope it warms up pretty soon. They say it's usually around 60 degrees down here. I wish the weather would behave itself.

  You wouldn't believe what we've been through just getting into the Army. Fingerprints, security forms, blood tests, etc. etc. We get up at 4:30 in the morning and at 5 we have breakfast.After that, we're on the move until noon when we have lunch. The afternoon is busy too until 4:30. After that we go to supper at 5:00. Tonite, for some odd reason, from 5:00 to 9:00 is free time. At 9:00 it's lights out, but believe me, you're ready for the sack long before then.I'm dead tired right now, and it's only 6:30.

  I got my hair cut today and you ought to see it. I can't call Dad bald anymore — I am too. We're required to get a haircut every 7 days.

Don't try to write to me until I send you my address. We're in what's called a Reception Station right now and we can write, but we can't receive letters. I should have my permanent address for boot camp by next week. At any rate, I'll send you my address as soon as I can. I'm bushed, so I think I'll say bye for now. Say hi to the kids and Lassie for me. Take care and may God bless.

love,

Tommie

PS. I miss you all —

* * *

On 30 September 1966, Tom graduated from the United States Army Primary Helicopter School (USAPHS), in Fort Wolters, Texas, which marked the first phase of flight school which had lasted from 14 May 1966 to 28 October 1966.

 United States Army Primary Helicopter School Fort Wolters, Texas

22 June 1966

Dear Mom & Dad,

I got your letters yesterday. I hope Bobby's wedding turned out to be okay. I wish him and Lee the very best of luck.

This week I have even less time to myself than before. It seems that they want to see what I can do in a leadership position. I am now a section leader for this week, and it's a pretty big job. I'll be getting graded on it, so I hope I'll do all right.I did pretty bad yesterday and the day before, so right now I'm pretty well discouraged. If I don't start flying a lot better pretty soon, I may as well throw in the towel and go back to infantry.

Well, at least the time out here seems to be going by fairly fast.Do you realize it's been almost 6 weeks already? Only 30 more to go, providing I don't end up washing out because of a flying deficiency.Well, today's another day — I hope I do a lot better today, or the whole bottom is going to drop out. Wish me luck!?!

We had an exam in aerodynamics today and I think I only missed one or two, so at least my academics seem to be okay, even if I can't fly right.

Judging from the way my handwriting is going uphill, it looks as though I'm going to have to start using lined stationery.

Well, I've got to be going. I'm sorry to be so short, but this job is keeping me going. Take care, write again soon and may God bless you all.

Love,

Demmie

P.S. I miss you all very much!

* * *

Letter from Fort Knox, Kentucky. They are training for Vietnam.

Fort Knox – 11 May 1967

  Dear Dad

  I haven't got too much time right now, so this is going to be pretty short. Enclosed you will find my share of what we talked about on the phone.

  Things have been pretty good around here, even though they manage to keep pretty doggone busy. It is now ten at night and I have been off duty for approximately fifteen minutes. In other words, I'm dead tired.

  Tell Mom that I wish her a very happy Mother's Day and say hito everyone for me. I've got to run, Dad, before I fall asleep sitting in this chair.

  Take care and may God bless ————

* * *

On 30 September 1967, just ten days before he left home for

Vietnam, Tom gave an engagement ring to his girlfriend, Veda. Here Tom (left) is pictured at a formal event at Fort Knox, just prior to deployment to Vietnam. Also pictured are Major James Marett (center) and WO John Shephardson (right)

Thomas Pueschel, James Marett, John Shephardson

Day 1, 10 October 1967 – Getting There

The sky was cloudy and the temperature in the mid-60s on a gloomy October morning in 1967. Soldiers from all over the country were milling around on the dock at the Oakland Army Base. Moored in the harbor was the USNS Nelson M. Walker, preparing for departure to Qui Nhon, South Vietnam at 1800 hours. By departure, over 5,300 soldiers would have boarded the old vessel.

GIs boarding 1966 (left; source: 1-22Infantry.org); USNS General Nelson M. Walker (right)

It was a slow procession onto the ship. Each soldier knew that they were bound for a war that they had only read about, in a foreign land that most knew little or nothing about. They were mostly just kids in their early twenties, some barely out of high school, and all, with an entire life to look forward to. The great majority of them had never been on a ship this size, and some might have never been on a boat at all. Their first battle would be a bout of seasickness, leaving them lining the rails for days.

Anxious as they must be, the soldiers didn't seem to show it. They were mostly quiet and orderly as they lined up single file, their gear on their shoulders as they readied to board the ship and find their place below deck.Many were thinking about the past, about those they were leaving behind, already missing them. They wondered about their future, the big uncertain future that lay before them, and if all the bad things said about Vietnam were true. Some were cool and casual, almost not bothered by it all, even anxious to get started, others fidgety and nervous. And for some it was a reality that hadn't sunk in yet. Each soldier, mired in their own thoughts and fears, knowing that this was a stressful beginning to a part of their lives they would never forget, if they were lucky enough to live through it.

Warrant Officer Thomas R. Pueschel was traveling with his entire unit, the 160 men of Troop C 7th Squadron 17th Air Cavalry, (C/7/17). He climbed the metal stairs and headed onto the ship. Tom had enlisted in 1965, partially because if he had not enlisted, there was a good chance he would have been drafted into the infantry. At least, by enlisting, he had some choice as to what he would be doing in the Army. He had talked about flying even as a young boy in Massachusetts. Now, at age 22, he was living that dream. He was flying helicopters for the Army and he loved flying helicopters. After basic training in Fort Polk, Louisiana, he had trained at the Army's Primary Helicopter School at Fort Wolters, Texas, and following that, at the Army Aviation School at Fort Rucker, Alabama. As for the flying, he was well prepared. As for whatever else came his way, only time would tell.

The 7th Squadron/17th Air Cavalry and the 3rd Squadron/17th Air Cav had been formed at Fort Knox, Kentucky. The two squadrons trained together, and now they were being deployed separately, going to different areas of Vietnam. They had boarded buses at dawn in Fort Knox for the 35-mile trip from Fort Knox to Standiford Field in Louisville, Kentucky, where they boarded a chartered flight bound for the West Coast and Oakland Army Base. From there, they were bussed to the dock and then boarded the USNS Walker as a group. There were no relatives there to see them off. Any send-offs had to have been done when leaving Fort Knox, in Standiford Field, or in hometowns across the country. Now, it was just a matter of moving around with your unit. Outside connections and relatives at home were on the back burner on this day. All that was there was a 20-man brass band giving them a royal sendoff.

Band playing to an empty parking lot, as troops look on from deck of USNS Walker

The commanding officer of the 7/17th was Lieutenant Colonel (LTC) Lawrence H. Johnson and he had left for Vietnam in an advanced party, leaving the XO (Executive Officer) Major Owen V. Haxton as acting commander. Major Haxton had deemed the 7/17th ready. "The effectiveness of the training program was confirmed by superior results obtained during the 7th Squadron's Army Training Test last July."

And the troops were further encouraged by a huge proclamation from the military command, "Ain't no question about it, we're gonna end the war!"

The USNS General Nelson M. Walker was one of many vessels that participated in the "steel bridge" from the United States to the war effort in Vietnam. She was 638 feet 11 inches long with a 75-foot beam and would steam west towards Vietnam at an estimated running speed of 19 knots (about 22 mph). She was an old ship, some might have called her a "rust bucket", having been built in 1944 and commissioned in April 1945 as the USS Admiral H. T. Mayo. Her first voyage in June 1945 was the transport of 5,819 released German-held prisoners of war from Le Havre, France, to Boston. It would be their first leg in the grand homecoming of Americans from WWII. In 1946, the Mayo would see her name changed and she was re-commissioned as the USAT General N. M. Walker. Later, she was refitted and designed to carry 3,700 troops at optimum load but she saw that number exceed 5,000 many times during her voyages.

Early in the Vietnam War, troop ships such as the USNS Upshur, Geiger, and Gordon carried two thirds of U.S. troops to Vietnam; later, most American troops traveled by air. (Source: Military Sea Transportation Service or MSTS.)

On this day in October 1967, some twenty-two years after her maiden voyage, the Walker would again be crowded and over capacity with over 5,000 aboard. This ship was bound for a different type of war than the battles fought in WWII. The enemy was more elusive, less defined, and the real purpose of being there, in Southeast Asia, less than clear.

No women were on board this ship, all men ready and able to go and fight for their country. While on the ship, the men would be under the command of Lieutenant Colonel (LTC) Christopher B. Sinclair. In addition to the military, 233 civilian marine officers and crewmen under the Master, Captain H.C. Petrosky, operated the ship. The entire trip took nearly 20 days.It steamed past the Hawaiian Islands, scheduled to make a stop in Okinawa before arriving in Vietnam.However, the ship was diverted from Okinawa and made its only port stop at Subic Bay, US Naval Air Station, in the Philippines before its eventual arrival in Vietnam. The primary reason for the diversion was Typhoon Dinah which was storming up through Japan and out into the Pacific. The ship skirted the edges of the typhoon that sometimes caused the 44' propellers of the ship to come out of the water as the Walker crested a wave. With Okinawa unavailable, the only other port able to accommodate a ship this size and its supply demands was Subic Bay.

With the ship so heavily loaded, to say life on board was close quarters would be an understatement. Quarters were so close as to be unbearable at times.

Hit the Rack! And not a very big rack it was. The canvas bunks (racks) were 6 feet long and just 2 feet wide, stacked 4-5 beds high and just 18 inches apart. Typically, 96 men to a room. So, sleeping wasn't all that easy. This confined, conditions were downright awful. But living onboard was even harder for some who were forced to "hot bunk." This meant, you got the rack for 12 hours and then someone else got it for 12 hours and so on. Luckily for the 7/17th Air Cav, they weren't one of those unfortunate groups.

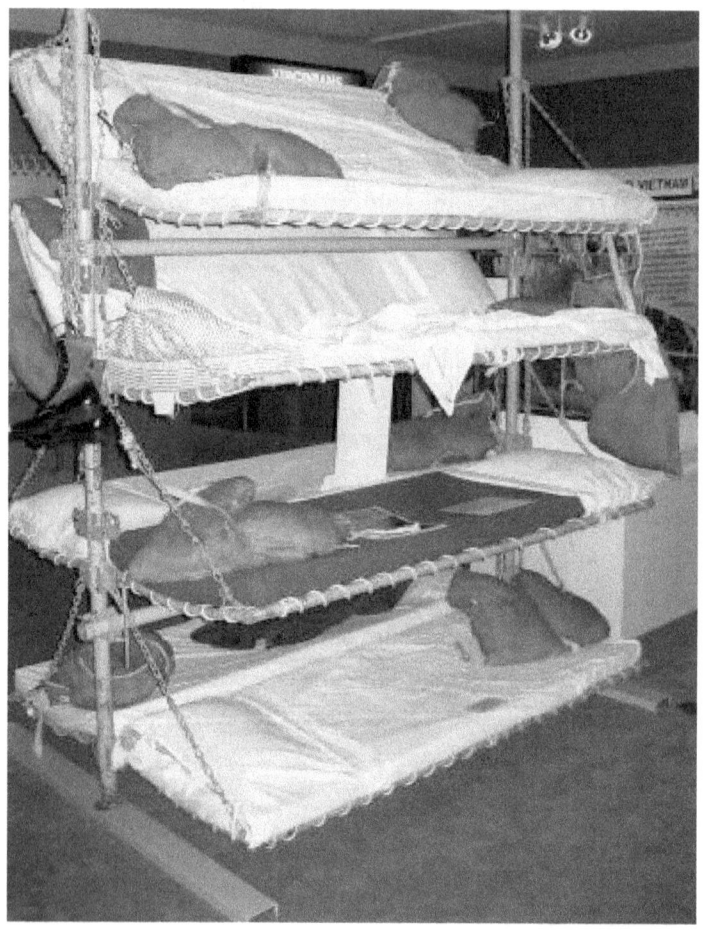

8-Man Berthing Unit (Source: Vietnam Graffiti project)

The weather on the trip varied from pleasant to scary while on the fringes of a hot and humid typhoon. There weren't many places to go on the ship, so above deck became many soldiers favorite landing spot. Above deck, you could stand near the stern of the ship and watch the wake or sit on deck and watch the day go by. The units on board had some drills but there was more slack time for the soldiers than at any other time in their service so far.Below deck there was cards, always cards, and more cards. Although the soldiers had been instructed not to gamble, they still gambled. And why not? They were headed for Vietnam, weren't they.

As for correspondence with those at home, soldiers could write as many letters home as they wanted to. But they couldn't send them, and they couldn't read any letters as there was no mail delivery or mail posting until the 25th when the ship docked in Subic Bay. At that stop, letters were collected at Purser's Square and then mailed at Subic Bay.

With over 5,300 guys in such a confined space, there were bound to be disagreements and fights, most times over nothing. Usually, they were broken up pretty quickly. But a fight was a fight and it was at least something to watch or maybe even participate in, once in a while.

The ship published the "Walker Report", the ship's newspaper, a seven- or eight-page, brochure-size paper which offered glimpses of recent news, sports, stories, and even included comics, crosswords, and other games. It also published the movie schedule for the day. The paper was "published daily, except Sundays, while at sea." It was really the only place aboard ship to get the news. It reported news of the war, the war that these guys were headed toward, and it was not always good news. It also reported the goings-on at home, politics and such, all done in just a few short sentences. In the Sports section of the 13 October issue, a soldier could read about the Cardinals beating the Red Sox in game seven of the 1967 World Series and could catch up on scores from the National

Football League.

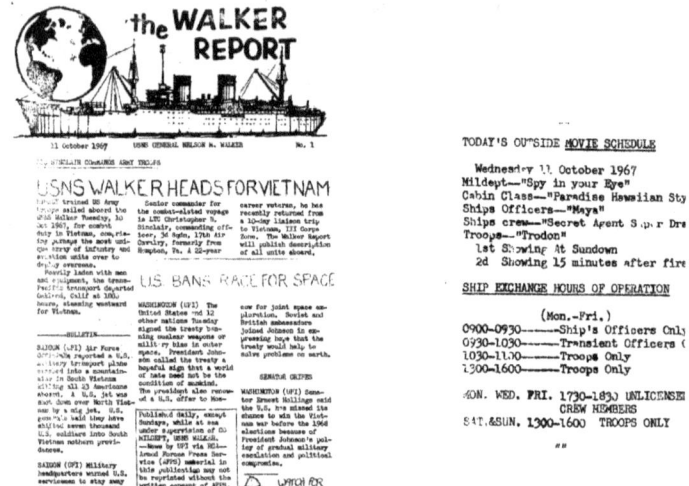

The Walker Report, 11 October 1967, p. 1 and p. 8 excerpt

Movies were shown almost every day, but many soldiers never got to see any of them because it was always very crowded and hard to get a spot where you could see the screen. For many soldiers, the boredom was indescribable.

As for the food, food on a ship of 5,000 doesn't offer a lot of variety or much of any special flavor. It was always bland at best and at times it seemed barely edible. As the voyage wore on and the ship approached Subic Bay in the Philippines, the food supplies, on top of being not of the good quality, also became in short supply.

The troops of the 7/17th were getting anxious as the last days on the ship seemed to last forever. "I can't wait to get up in the air again, I also can't wait to get to Vietnam. All I've heard since I started flying was Nam is like this, and that, and I want to find out for myself. If everything goes alright, we should be in Nam tomorrow afternoon.Went to flick tonight and Silencers. 350 days to go." (Source: The History of the 7th Armored Squadron, 17th Air Cavalry-Rick Schoeny Diary entry 26 October 1967).

So, this was life on the USNS General Walker. The soldiers were crowded beyond imagination; the food was middling at best, but bad most of the time; the sleeping accommodations not very accommodating; and they had to cope with boredom, seasickness, cramped spaces with no place to go, and the 5,000-mile journey would last nearly three weeks.

The ship layover in Subic Bay was about 18 hours. Initially the men were not allowed ashore, but then somebody realized there were thousands of soldiers and the military couldn't arrest all of them so there was a mass disembarkation. In the end, there were many stories about that stopover, many which cannot be told.

From Subic Bay, South Vietnam was a short two days away. There, the troops would disembark in country, at Qui Nhon Army Airfield.

Arrival in Qui Nhon, Vietnam 27 October 1967

One of the soldiers aboard the Walker on that trip echoed the thoughts of many:

"My theory is that the purpose of cramming us all into that rusty scow was to make us mad enough to kill – and then they handed us guns."

Day 9, 18 October 1967 – "Ease my unquiet soul."

As U.S. Army Warrant Officer Thomas R. Pueschel crossed the Pacific Ocean on board the transport ship USNS General Walker, en route to Vietnam in October 1967, many thoughts buzzed through his head. In this letter, he speaks in an "off guard" moment, to his worried parents:

18 October 1967

Dear Mom & Dad,

How do you like my little friend over there in the corner? I think he's kind of cute, and, besides, he seems to agree pretty much with my views on Viet Nam. I think I'll adopt him as my mascot, as a matter of fact.

18 October 1967

Dear Mom & Dad,

How do you like my little friend over there in the corner? I think he's kind of cute, and, besides he seems to agree pretty much with my views on Viet Nam. I think I'll adopt him as my mascot as a matter of fact.

We crossed what they call the International Dateline last night, and time moved ahead twenty-four hours just like that! Yesterday was Monday, the 16th of October, and today is Wednesday, the 18th. How's that for sour pickles??? God! I've got enough trouble just keeping the date straight as it is, and then they had to go and pull this one on me. It's enough to make a guy want to join the Flat Earth Society!!! Who knows, next they might tell us that if we cross the equator, we will lose the upper half of the day. Come to think of it, that wouldn't be such a bad idea after all – it would cut my tour in Viet Nam in half and I'd be on my way home six months sooner. Fat chance of that ever happening, though, but a guy can always dream.

By the way, what do you think of the idea of Veda and I coming up to Massachusetts to live after my hitch in the Army, so I can finish school at UMass? Actually, it was kind of her idea as she would like to see me finish just as much as I want to. I was also thinking of trying out some night courses back in the U.S. during the remainder of my hitch after Viet Nam. I am hoping that I will get assigned to Fort Wolters as an instructor when I get back, and I could probably attend Dallas University a couple of nights a week. I am hoping to get enough college behind me so that I will be able to get a job as a high school teacher or a college instructor later on. That is one profession that has a lot of merits, and if I could only tie flying in with it I would be riding high in the wagon! Who knows, though, maybe I'll end up as an airline jockey or something along that line. These are all sort of random thoughts right now as I have a lot to go through before I can make any definite plans, and I am hoping that by the end of my hitch with Uncle Sam I will know better what I want to do and will have pretty much decided on a course of action.

There is one thing that has been increasingly invading my thoughts that I feel I have to get off my chest. I have spoken about it to Veda, somewhat in some of my, so to speak, off guard moments. I did not want to worry her and neither do I want to worry you more than you are already, but I've got to let it out. To put it in plain words without beating around the bush, I am plain scared. I know a lot of it stems from mere anticipation of the unknown, but it is yet something more. I am not afraid to die, if that be in the cards, but I am afraid that I will not be able to do what I have to do. It is going to be a dirty, messy job and if I had my way, I probably would have no part of it. I've been thinking and wondering if I have what it takes to kill another human being. All my life, you and the church have taught me, 'Thou shalt not kill' and yet, I now find myself on a ship which is taking me to a place where I will be expected to do just that. It is a battle that has been raging in me for many months now, and I cannot find what seems to be an answer, and I guess I will not until that final test comes when I come face to face with my enemy and have to tighten my finger on the trigger and blast the breath of life in an instant from the body of a fellow man. I know it will be him or me, and I think that I may be able to do it, but the thought still frightens me terribly. Can I really take the life of a man, and afterwards, can I really justify that act by attributing it to my own instincts for self-preservation? I don't expect you to answer my questions, but it seems to help to 'talk it out' and I know that sometime somewhere, with God's help, I will find the answers and ease my unquiet soul. It is something I will have to work out for myself.

25

Well, I guess this is it, for now.There really isn't too much you can write about on this trip. Take care and may God bless ——-.

PS. If you get around to putting that thing in the paper, how about sending Veda a copy – she likes to collect things like that. Ok?"

These were the thoughts of the young soldier trying to work things out in his own mind, fighting his own doubts, following his own sense of duty, preparing for war, and trying to ease his "unquiet soul."

Fellow pilot and friend John Shephardson who was a classmate of Tom's throughout flight school, and served with him during his time in Vietnam, had this to say about Tom:

"For whatever it's worth: your brother (Tom) was a great guy. I have to tell you that through the years I have often thought of the group we were in. Some of us were running away from something, some of us were dragged off the streets kicking and screaming and some of us, like Tom, were there out of a sense of duty. Some of us were street punks, some were farm boys, some were adventurers and some, like Tom, were artists at heart. There were 3 people including Tom who I always thought deserved to be elsewhere as they were more sensitive (artists at heart). Sadly all 3 have passed while some of us live on. Life is neither predictable nor fair. Tom deserved a longer life and you could even say he earned it by his "time in hell". I'm just sorry that he is no longer around. I thought you might like to know that."

In February 1942, just two months after Pearl Harbor in WWII, Tom's Uncle Walter was on a similar journey and thought of home and those far away as an American soldier in the service of his country. Walter Gerhardt sent this picture and note home to his sister Erna (Gerhardt) Pueschel (eventually Tom's mother). It was a different war in different times, but still another soldier missing home but bound to duty. The soldier was proud to send this picture home with his own thoughts of home and those far away in the written inscription.

"There comes a time in every man's life where his heart turns towards thoughts of home and those far away. This is just a small remembrance given in the true spirit as an American soldier in the service of his country."

Tom's Uncle Walter Gerhardt writes home, February 1942

And then there were those of us who weren't required to serve and chose not to. Like Tom's brother, Larry:

"I am Tom's brother. I did not go to Vietnam. My draft number in the 1969 draft lottery was 356, way too high to ever have to serve in the military or even report for a physical. I didn't even have to think about it. I'd gotten a free pass. It was a time when all of us young 19-year-old kids worried about going to Vietnam but once I pulled that high number, I didn't have to worry, except on behalf of my brother. The closest I got to the war was watching that damn lottery on TV in the lounge of my dormitory with a whole lot of my classmates, all hoping for the best. Instead of fighting, I never even had to go to some draft board and stand on a cold floor in my underwear waiting my turn to be examined by some military doctor. I got to finish college and live a life in a different world, far apart from cannons firing and bullets flying. I would never get PTSD from military action. I participated in protests against the war. I was just a kid. We were all kids. As I have grown older, a big part of me feels regret over not having to serve like others did. It almost felt as though I was given a hall pass on one of life's many tests. The more I read and re-read my brother's letters and heard from him and his compatriots and friends, and the more I learned about the war and what these soldiers were up against, I could understand the great sacrifice these men had to make. It's a sacrifice I didn't get at the time, but I get it now. And I thank them for it. All of them. Most Heartily."

Life is short and precious enough not to have to think about an instance where you have to "tighten my finger on the trigger and blast the breath of life in an instant from the body of a fellow man." It's agonizing what we humans are sometimes asked to do and even more agonizing what we are capable of when the metal hits the road. We have to fight each other, it's ingrained, no matter what the cause. Wars are forever.

Day 23, 1 November 1967 – "Sure ruined a nice dream I was having!"

Nighttime in Pleiku. The night sky was clear, starry. The temperature was a brisk 51 degrees and, compared to where it had been all day, hanging in the mid-80s, it felt really cold. The tent wasn't great but it could have been worse..."at least it wasn't a pup." There were eight cots set up on the tent's wooden floor, and some space. Not a lot of space, but more than on the ship. A perimeter had been established around the camp, with guards stationed, and eyes on lookout. It was still confining but not like on the ship. And the solid ground beneath their feet felt good. Each of the soldiers was given only two blankets but they made due, as soldiers do.

Tent City, Camp Enari — Pleiku, Vietnam

The light in the tent wasn't very good but at least it was a light. They didn't have lights in the tents at all when they first got there, just a few short days ago, but now they did. A group of soldiers, including a West Point graduate in Engineering, commandeered some wire and strung it to the main power source, and then strung a couple of bulbs into each of the tents. In the coming days, each soldier worked to make the camp better and it was coming together.

The light was bright enough so that a young soldier could write a letter…and WO Tom Pueschel was finally ready to sit down and write a letter home. It had been about two weeks since he last wrote home and he knew they would be looking for one. In the back of his mind, he hoped they wouldn't be too worried.

Wednesday, 1 Nov. 1967

   Dear Mom & Dad,

   Greetings and salutations once again from your prodigal son in Viet Nam! Here at Pleiku, we are now just starting the winter season, just as you are back home.It was fairly cool today with temperatures around eighty degrees, but most of the time we average from around ninety to ninety-five degrees during the day - eight hours. It gets downright chilly around here at night, though, with a temperature averaging around fifty degrees or so. All in all, though, it makes it pretty comfortable to sleep with just a couple of blankets to cover you, even though we only have an eight-man tent to sleep in. There are only seven of us in my tent, so there is plenty of room anyway.

   So far it has been pretty quiet around here with only a few exceptions. Most of the time, however, it doesn't even seem as if we are actually in a combat area. A couple of nights ago, we had a couple of mortar rounds land near our compound, but that wasn't much to worry about. They didn't do any damage, to speak of, but they sure ruined a nice dream I was having! Otherwise, we haven't been doing much except setting up our base camp and getting acquainted with our surroundings.

   I have already received a couple of your letters – thanks for writing. I can't begin to tell you how much it means to receive mail from home. Could you do me a favor, though? There are a few things that are hard to come by around here, and I was wondering if you could send me some of them. They are as follows: flash-light batteries (C & D size – for my flashlight and tape-recorder), writing paper and envelopes, scissors, masking tape, paint (enamel – red, yellow, blue, black, white, brown), needle and thread, and cookies and chocolate. Ok? (I kind of wish you could also put Veda in a carton and send her too, but I don't guess that would be practical, would it.Besides, I wouldn't want her to get hurt – it's bad enough that I have to be here sticking my neck out.)

So far, the plan, so to speak, for my unit is to stay here at our base camp in Pleiku for at least another month and a half or so, (training and such), and then one of the troops (A, B, or C) will go north of here to a forward combat area near the DMZ for a period of about six weeks. At the same time, one of the other troops will be staying here, while the last goes south, also for about six weeks or so. After that, each troop will again be rotated, one north, one south, and one to the base camp here. That means that we will only be spending a maximum of twelve weeks in the field in one whack, and then, six weeks here where we can sort of rest up again. It'll be a lot better than living in a pup tent for a year anyway, and once we get some wooden, semi-permanent buildings built here, it won't be bad at all. They say we will even be able to have maid service!!!

Oh, yes, here's a little news that will probably make Dad a little envious – liquor, Canadian Club, for example, costs $1.80 a quart here.How's that compared to prices in the states? It doesn't do me all that much good though, 'cause I rarely drink, and when I do, it isn't very much. I bet if I bought a quart now, I would probably have some of that same bottle left six months from now!

Well, I guess this is it for now. Don't worry about me – I'll get along alright – I always have, and I always will. Ich kann nicht anders!

May God bless you all and keep you safe in His care.

33

May God bless you all and keep you safe in His care.

Love,

Tom

PS. In case you're wondering about the paint I want – that's how I've been making a little extra money. I've made $21 dollars so far, and that averages out at about $3 per hour of work. Pretty good, huh? I'm going to need all the money I can get if I'm going to get married when I get back!!!"

Tom finished the letter, addressed the envelope, and got it ready to mail. Then he lay back in his cot. He needed his rest and stretching out felt good.

He looked around the tent and wondered how long he would be in one of these things. He never did like camping. And from the trip over the ocean, he had found out he wasn't too keen about ships either. And then after that, there was the grind of the trip to Pleiku up through the mountains in those dam trucks. That was no easy process.

Tom stirred in his cot. It was his first official night in Vietnam. He didn't know what was coming next. What would be or what would not be. The night air surrounded him in his restless sleep and his eyes blinked open. He stared into the darkness. He sure would be glad to be flying again.

A few days earlier – 27 October 1968

Many of the soldiers were up on deck during the next part of their journey. They knew they were nearing Vietnam and they were watching to see its coastline. It had been nearly two days since they left Subic Bay and the sighting of land was close. It was early evening, around 5:30 when they spotted it, the land that was the dark silhouette of the Republic of Vietnam. It would still take another two hours before the ship would make its way to port and harbor.

Around 7:30 PM, the ship anchored in Qui Nhon Harbor. Only one more night onboard and then it was Vietnam time. From the harbor, the 5300 soldiers onboard could see the lights of the city Qui Nhon and Qui Nhon Airfield. It had been a long seventeen days since they had left Oakland, California way back on the 10th of October. As they watched now, from the deck of the Walker, they could see flashes and hear the distinct thundering of artillery rounds in the distance. Their journey on the USNS General Walker was nearly over. And they were In Vietnam. Officially, physically, and mentally, they were here – the Republic of Vietnam (RVN). One soldier wrote in his dairy, *"It's kind of weird and frightening looking at the dark coast and watching artillery rounds going off."* (Source: The History of the 7th Armored Squadron, 17th Air Cavalry).

American forces were allied with the South Vietnam army or ARVN (Army of the Republic of Vietnam). North Vietnam was composed of the VC (Viet Cong), and NVA (North Vietnamese Army)/ PAVN (People's Army of Vietnam). The VC were guerrilla fighters and the NVA/PAVN troops were regular army of North Vietnam.

While docked in harbor, the ship had to be protected from attack by underwater sappers who were elite VC/NVA combatants and swimmers, capable of attacking ships, bridges, and bases in lightning raids.During that last night on the Walker,

U.S. patrol boats were seen and heard circling the ship and dropping concussion charges and precision grenades into the water as a way to deter the sappers.

At daylight on 28 October 1967, the ship pulled up to the dock to begin unloading. With gangplanks lowered, the soldiers filed out of the ship, giving the old gal one long last kiss goodbye as they set their feet in the steamy port city of Qui Nhon, Vietnam.

The Convoy and Highway 19 - the road to Pleiku

By 9:15 AM, the troops had all debarked the ship and begun the process of being loaded with full gear onto large 2 ½-ton military transport trucks. There were about 8-10 men in each truck. They sat on wooden seats, and the trucks had no springs, and there was lots of dust. It was no picnic, but the soldiers were happy to at least be off that damned boat and finally getting on with what was to come. They were headed to a base camp in Pleiku, a town in the central highlands of Vietnam. They would be in the trucks for a good ten hours making the 110-mile journey on Highway 19 from Qui Nhon through An Khe Pass to Pleiku. The troops of the 7/17th were supplied with guns but due to supply problems, were only provided with three rounds of ammunition.

Convoy en route to Pleiku (left); Kids Saluting Convoy in Qui Nhon
(Source: G.Ross video)

As the convoy trucked through the city of Qui Nhon they could see kids playing, waving, and even saluting. At least some of the population appeared to welcome them but most just watched. They passed by a beautiful church in downtown Qui Nhon, big gold crosses shining in the sun. They passed farmer after farmer in the fields and paddies. The farmers continued to work, with little reaction to the convoy on the road nearby. They mostly just kept their heads down.

Highway 19 was the main road connecting the coastal region of Qui Nhon and the Central Highlands. It was rough, narrowly paved, and very dusty. It started in the lowlands, areas of mostly farming, and then wound its way into the upper elevations. The trip was slow and steady as the trucks rambled along at about 10-15 mph. As they reached the highlands, the road was often steep, full of turn-backs, and it was narrow through the woods and jungle.

This was not safe passage. The terrain provided the PAVN (People's Army of Vietnam) and VC with prime ambush locations. The An Khe Pass was one of the most dangerous areas along the route and the road snaked its way through "Ambush Alley" east of the Mang Yang Pass, which was the site of the massacre of French Union troops in 1954. Incidents occurred on this stretch of road on an almost daily basis, and it had been said that *"...in the high mountain passes you can still hear whispering in the wind the ghosts of past battles that have been fought along this road."* (Source: "Vietnam's Route 19: 20 Year of Ambush Warfare," published in the Kent Ohio Record-Courier, 12 Feb 1970 edition)

The troops were warned of the potential for ambush and to be ready for it. The 7/17th had but three rounds apiece and the trucks were open, leaving the troops highly vulnerable to attack. However, the convoy was long, maybe too long, discouraging the enemy from even attempting an ambush. No ambush would come that day, and they made their way to their new base camp in Pleiku, unharmed and feeling lucky. The supply convoy following the same route the very next day suffered a different fate; they were ambushed, and the attack had to be repelled.

Pleiku – Camp Enari, the Tent City

The convoy arrived at the base camp, Camp Enari, which was about 8 miles (12 km) southeast of the city of Pleiku, on the 28th of October around 7-8 at night. It was dark and extremely cold. The troops tumbled out of the convoy and were issued a cot, given two blankets, some c-rations, and assigned to a tent.

As daybreak broke, the soldiers could now see where they were – a lot of red mud or red dust, depending on the day. That was Camp Enari. The camp was a sea of tents with a number of units clustered together, set up in an open field with little or no trees and a lot of mud and dirt and sandbags in between. A heliport and maintenance area were in close proximity to the tent city. The unit worked together for the next few weeks to get the camp in order. It became operational sometime in mid-November. In Vietnam, it was said, there was always some kind of construction going on.

On the horizon, in good view from the camp, was Dragon Mountain (Núi Hàm Rồng), and Camp Enari was also known as Dragon Mountain Base Camp and Hensel Airfield.

Camp Enari was named for 1st Lieutenant Mark Enari, the first 4th Infantry Division member awarded the Silver Star (posthumously) in Vietnam, who was killed in action on 2 December 1966. Hensel Airfield was named after WO-1 Ernest Hensel, a 10th Cavalry helicopter gunship pilot who was killed in action on 17 February 1967. (Source: Wikipedia)

Tom's unit was C Troop, 7th Squadron, 17th Air Cavalry, (C/7/17).About a month after they had arrived at Camp Enari, that troop would go North to Chu Lai and become attached to the Americal Division, where, come spring time, it would be re-designated as F Troop, 8th Cavalry. He would serve the rest of his time in Vietnam with F Troop and be stationed in Chu Lai.

His stay in Pleiku lasted approximately one month.

Follow the Yellow Road — Qui Nhon to Pleiku to Chu lai

Day 23, 1 November 1967 – "I'll shoot a few for you too, ok?"

Tommie Pueschel, Bill Utley, and Johnny Zokowski—what a trio! Best friends growing up. Always up to something, they went through Junior High and High School together in Holyoke, Massachusetts and had been good friends ever since. They would be friends for life. Tom wrote this letter to Bill Utley just a few days after arriving in Vietnam. He wanted to tell him about Veda and the "sparkles on her finger"!

1 November 1967

Dear Bill,

I received your letter yesterday afternoon – it was great to hear from you again.

So you went and did it, huh? I guess condolences – I mean congratulations, are in order. I guess you haven't received my letter to you with my earth-shattering news. Remember Veda? Well, she's now officially my fiancé, sparkles on her finger, and notice in the paper and everything!!! How's that grab you? Now all I have to do is get home in one piece, but i think I'm stubborn enough to do it.

By the way, my APO number is 9—-2. Use it just like a zip code.

Things have been pretty quiet around here lately, and at times, it's actually hard to believe we're in a war zone. That'll change pretty soon, though, as my troop is slated for a little jaunt for a couple months up north – about a mile and a half from the DMZ. There goes the Army again pulling the Marines' chestnuts out of the fire.

Damn, there goes another 105-howitzer making noise again. I don't mind our artillery giving Charley a little hell now and then, but did they have to put that damn gun so close to my tent?? I guess they're a little mad though; we had a couple mortar rounds land near our compound – not enough to do any damage to speak of, but it sure scared the hell out of me. It's not exactly the best way to wake up, and besides, they managed to ruin a real sexy dream!

Well, give my regards to Marge and you both have my congratulations and best wishes. I wish I could be there for the wedding, but I kind of doubt if I can swing it. Thanks for thinking of me for the best man. Good luck, anyway, and take care.

By the way, guess who else is here at Pleiku with us – the 69th Armor Bttn!! How's that for a unit?

Well, Bill, take care and stay happy, and I'll shoot a few for you too, ok?

Bill Utley was commissioned as a 2nd Lieutenant (2LT) in the Infantry in June 1968 out of Syracuse University having been part of the ROTC program. Bill would go to Vietnam in

August 1969 as a company platoon leader, company executive officer, and Battalion S-3 Air (Air ops). He served there with Charlie, Echo (Heavy Weapons), and Headquarters Company, 1st Battalion, 501st Infantry Regiment, 101st Airborne Division (Airmobile). At about his 10-month mark, he was in a Huey that got shot down while out delivering replacement signal operating instructions to teams in the field. He suffered heavy shrapnel wounds and was evacuated out of Vietnam through Japan and then back home. He recovered from extensive injuries and would later serve with the Secret Service.

Note: The *"69th Armor Bttn!! How's that for a unit?"* that Tom referred to, in the second to last sentence of his letter, was a tank battalion. Tanks were not a major weapon in Vietnam because of the often-soggy ground conditions. But they were there, providing valuable support on roadways, in urban areas, and in places with harder surfaces.

M48A3 Patton Tank of 1st Battalion, 69th Armor, in Pleiku in 1966
(Source: Wikipedia)

43

Day 38, 16 November 1967 – "weirdo 'crackpot' youngsters"

Tom's Uncle Walter and Aunt Esther sent this letter to Tom's parents, Erna and Dick Pueschel:

Thursday a.m.

Dear Erna, Dick, + family —

Thanks for your letter – at the same time we received a beautiful letter from Tommy. It was a surprise & reached us in 4 days. We should save this letter and reread now and then. It makes us proud to know him as our nephew. Surely, this world should be filled with many more like him. Every time I read in the paper and see these weirdo, 'crackpot' youngsters in action I'll remember Tommy, & thank God his hand is at the helm helping the nation in its agony at a critical time. It made us think, and we cried a bit as he expressed his hopes + fears – his doubts. Surely, God, in his wisdom & compassion, must hear his words and help him see his job thru to a successful end. I wish I had more eloquence to tell him in words how deeply he touched us, & how very much we wanted to tell him how much we cared and prayed for his safety. He probably writes the same to you. How truly he and Veda deserve a good marriage & life – so he can carry the same philosophy over to the children they may have. How happy he must make you to call him 'son'.

Enclosed is another article written by soldiers on requests in packages they receive. Walter says I may be a pest to you, but they help me – I want to send one this week.Hope he gets it by Thanksgiving. They suggest mailing by SAM for quick delivery.

Enclosed are ....<personal part of the letter not shown>...

More again – dearest love and best regards – Lovingly,

Walter & Esther

Tom's Uncle Walter was a veteran, stationed in England during World War II.

As Aunt Esther wrote this letter, anti-war protests were occurring all over America. In contrast, competing counter-protests in support of the war were dwindling, weak, and poorly attended. By 1967 the anti-war movement was in full bloom and growing every day. The war was coming home, nearer and nearer to families' doorsteps, as more people knew someone who had been there, or was there now, or on the way there soon. The television coverage was intense and the images depressing. The death toll alarming. The country was becoming more anxious.

On Saturday, October 21st, the biggest anti-war protest to date occurred, called the March on the Pentagon. In Washington, DC, a crowd of over 100,000 protesters gathered at the Lincoln Memorial. The crowd in the March on the Pentagon was no longer just "weirdo crackpot youngsters" and anti-war radicals. The protest movement had become more diverse as every-day students, middle-class professionals, parents and grandparents, clergyman, black activists, celebrities, and veterans joined in protesting the war.

45

The crowd was energized by a concert from protest singer and counter-culturist Phil Ochs. The words from his song, *"I ain't marching anymore"* echoed through the crowd.

Call it peace or call it treason
Call it love or call it reason
But I ain't marching anymore
No, I ain't marching anymore

The concert was followed by fiery anti-establishment and anti-war speeches, some of which were laced with profanity and insult. From the Lincoln Memorial, about 50,000 of the protesters marched across the Memorial Bridge to the Pentagon where they were confronted by U.S. Marshalls and American soldiers. Tear gas and rifle butts were used to control the crowd. The protesters faced the troops for hours until they were dispersed sometime near midnight. Over 682 arrests and 47 injuries to protesters, soldiers, and U.S. marshals alike.

Protests like this continued to occur all across the country. The National Mobilization Committee to End the War in Vietnam (the MOBE) had been formed in November 1966 to organize large demonstrations against the war such as the March on the Pentagon.

At the University of Massachusetts in Amherst, a freshman student, Larry Pueschel, first heard the music of protest singer and songwriter, Phil Ochs, and was fascinated with his song of apathy, *"A Small Circle of Friends."* Like all other full-time students, he had a 2-S Student Deferment, which would keep him out of the draft and Vietnam as long as he was a full-time student with enough credit hours. A student who would drop below the 11-credit line would be heading to their draft board in short order. And nobody wanted to go there.

The Students for a Democratic Society (SDS) had a faction at UMass and began holding protests against Dow Chemical because of their part in the production of the hellfire firebomb,

Napalm. One of its members was a UMass student living on the same dormitory floor with Larry. While his brother was bravely fighting in Vietnam, he was hearing the voices of protest across the nation and at times they made a lot of sense to him.

Veterans Marching (Source: Washington Post) Protesters Crossing Memorial Bridge

Protesters at the Pentagon (Source: billofrights.org)

Singer/Song-Writer Phil Ochs

I Ain't Marching Anymore - by Phil Ochs
Oh, I marched to the battle of New Orleans
At the end of the early British wars
The young land started growing
The young blood started flowing
But I ain't marching anymore

For I've killed my share of Indians
In a thousand different fights
I was there at the Little Big Horn
I heard many men lying, I saw many more dying
But I ain't marching anymore

It's always the old to lead us to the wars
It's always the young to fall
Now look at all we've won with the saber and the gun
Tell me, is it worth it all?

For I stole California from the Mexican land
Fought in the bloody Civil War
Yes, I even killed my brothers
And so many others
But I ain't marching anymore

For I marched to the battles of the German trench
In a war that was bound to end all wars
Oh, I must have killed a million men
And now they want me back again
But I ain't marching anymore

It's always the old to lead us to the wars
Always the young to fall
Now look at all we've won with the saber and the gun
Tell me, is it worth it all?

For I flew the final mission in the Japanese skies
Set off the mighty mushroom roar
When I saw the cities burning
I knew that I was learning
That I ain't marching anymore

Now the labor leader's screamin'
When they close the missile plants
United Fruit screams at the Cuban shore
Call it peace or call it treason
Call it love or call it reason
But I ain't marching anymore
No, I ain't marching anymore

Day 48, 26 November 1967 – Chu Lai

Whup...whup...whup...whup...so went the "thickness noise" of the blades of the UH-1C helicopters headed up north to the Chu Lai Air Base. On the 26th of November, just three days after Thanksgiving, C troop was told that they were moving up North to I Corps and would be attached to the Americal Division (23rd Infantry). No dusty trucks for this trip, the troop made the approximate 130-mile trip flying their own helicopters. Other equipment was moved via C-130 aircraft and by tanks or transport vehicles.

Once at Chu Lai, building the base camp began all over again. The work had begun right away upon arrival at the Chu Lai Air Base. The troop graduated from the tent city of Pleiku to wood-frame huts in Chu Lai. They installed showers, renovated buildings, put up new latrines and built bunkers for perimeter defense. By 4 December, the maintenance area was well established, and the troops and the Ky Hia Heliport were ready for combat. The FOB (Forward Operating Base) at Chu Lai was Hawk Hill or Hill 29, was located about 15 miles north of Chu Lai at the entrance to the Que Son Valley. Troop C would operate out of there most of the time.

Note (per Wikipedia): Chu Lai Air Base was a military airport in Chu Lai, Vietnam, operated by the United States Marine

Corps between 1965 and 1970. It was located near Tam Kỳ city, the largest city in Quảng Nam Province. It was abandoned after the end of the Vietnam War, and reopened as Chu Lai International Airport in 2005.

Two Pilots, Terry Rippy and Tom Pueschel share a moment

Day 54, 2 December 1967 – "Here he comes again."

"... someone's got to do it, ... not the only one who'd rather be somewhere else. ... worse places to be than here at Chu Lai."

2 December 1967

Dear Mom & Dad,

Well, another new month started, and another month closer to going home. I wonder if they will try a Christmas truce again this year. If they do, I hope it turns out better than it did last year. With my luck, I'll probably get stuck flying patrol along the D.M.Z. on Christmas or New Year's Eve! it'd be just like the Army to pull some stunt like that.

We have started fixing up our living quarters, and believe it or not, they are actually starting to look half-way decent. We've even got our own back porch with a view of the Pacific Ocean – screened in, no less!!! Now, all we need is for our mail to catch up with us, and then things might be almost bearable. Somehow, though, I just flat-out don't like this country and even less, having to be here, But I guess someone's got to do it, and I'm not the only one who'd rather be somewhere else. I guess there could be worse places to be than here at Chu Lai.

'Here he comes again, head high and smilin'
  shakin down the world, playin' it cool.
  He smiles as though he's never been
  Hunted by the crowds, beaten by all the fools.
  Think of all the men who never knew the answers
  Think of all those who never cared.
  Still there are some who ask why
  Who want to know, and dare to try
  Every now and then we meet that kind of man
  Here he comes again and now he's gone.'

On that point, I shall now depart for the time being. Take care and may God bless. Stay happy!!

Love,

Our

In the middle of a war, Tom seemed to question the reasons for this war that he's in, as he recalled the lyrics of the song, *"Here he Comes Again"* by Rod McKuen, one of his favorite artists. He wrote them down in his letter home.

The last phrase of the song says, *"Here he comes again and now he's gone,"* could simply mean that no answers were coming for those *"who ask why"* and *"dare to try"*. At least, not anytime soon.

"Here he comes again" was sung by McKuen in his 1971 Christmas album titled *"New Carols for Christmas - The Rod McKuen Christmas Album"* but was originally created as a poem

in the 1960s. McKuen was an award-winning writer, singer, and composer but his greatest fame was that of a poet. His books of poetry sold in the millions, and its themes included love, optimism, the natural world and spirituality.

His website proclaims, "It doesn't matter who you love, or how you love, but that you love."

Rod McKuen 1971 Christmas Album

Day 54, 2 December 1967 – "That is one hairy experience, by the way."

A letter to Bill Utley. And asking permission to return fire.

2 December 1967

Dear Bill,

Greetings and salutations from Chu Lai, Vietnam! I hope you can keep up with my moving around 'cause I sure can't!

By the way my new address is now:

—WO Thomas R Pueschel

—C Troop 7th Sqdn 17th Cav.

—Americal Division

—APO San Francisco, Calif. 96374

As you can see, I am now attached to the Americal Division, and these guys flat-out don't fool around, and now that we are away from the squadron, we don't either! Yesterday, we received some automatic weapons fire from inside one of the villages, so we leveled the village, and I mean that literally! Up here, it's not like it was down in Pleiku, when we had to first <u>ask permission</u> to <u>return fire</u> and then receive permission when it was too damn late to do any good anyway. That can be a magnitudinously large pain in the rectal cleavage, if you know what I mean! They sure seemed awfully glad to see my troop get here, and they put us to work on *our second day in this area. Things have a way of getting pretty hectic, and awfully damn noisy around here. I was just wondering how long it will take me, once I am back in the states, to get used to not walking around with a loaded weapon under my left arm and how long it will take for me to stop jumping at every sound that sounds like gunfire or "incoming mail." That is one hairy experience, by the way – it sounds like the whole world is coming down around your ears.*

I've got to run – take care, stay happy, and if you can't be good, be careful!

Tom

P.S. Hurry up on over and help me give 'em hell!!!

Day 55, December 1967 - Chu Lai RVN by TRP

The young artist at work, creating what he is seeing...

Chu Lai, RVN by TRP (Thomas R. Pueschel) December 1967

Day 55, 3 December 1967 – "Say a little prayer and then be on my way."

The war in Chu Lai got nastier every day, as a good friend was hit and there was nothing Tom could do but "say a little prayer and then be on my way."

3 December 1967

Dear Mom & Dad,

Greetings and salutations from Chu Lai! I finally found out for sure about Dave Bressem. He is still alive – what's left of him, that is. It seems he was helping some people out of a burning aircraft when it blew up and took away half his face and burned the whole side of his body. From what I could find out, he was patched up in a hospital in Tokyo, and is now, I think, back home in the states. From what I could gather, he was pretty badly burned, has lost one eye, and will not regain full use of his arm or leg, but at least he is still alive, and that's a big load off my mind. It's pretty rough and he has my sympathy, but I have learned to expect things like this, and when they do, I say a little prayer and then be on my way. It may sound kind of hard & cold, but that is the way it has to be over here, for next time it could be you! So you feel a little sorry, and you hope that when the next time comes, that you will be able to say: 'Thank God it wasn't me,' again. War is a nasty thing, and the more I see of it, the nastier it gets, and I feel as I am perhaps becoming very much older and a little more nastier myself right along with it.

I've got to run – I've got an early mission tomorrow and it's quite late already.

Take care and may God bless.

Stay happy!
Love,
Du

That was Day 55 (Day 34 'in country'). It didn't take a long time in a combat zone to turn a person a little nastier. "War is a nasty thing, and the more I see of it, the nastier it gets, and I feel as I am perhaps become very much older and a little more nastier myself right along with it."

David Bressem, CWO2 B Troop, 1st Squadron, 9th Cavalry Regiment, 1st Cavalry Division

David Bressem survived the explosion of the burning aircraft, but his road to recovery was long and arduous. After being medevacked out of the field, he spent a few weeks in a field hospital in Vietnam and a few weeks in a hospital in Japan before being transported back to the States. He would spend over a year in Walter Reed Hospital before being discharged in 1969.

David Bressem in Vietnam. (Source: Veterans' History Project – Cathedral High School)

David Bressem had joined the Army right out of High School at 18-years-old. He enlisted because he knew he would be drafted and by enlisting this gave him the opportunity to have some choice of what he would be doing in the Army.After months of basic training and helicopter training, he was sent to Vietnam and arrived 'in country' at age 19. He had one thought about his training. "It's not normal for people to know how to kill people." And that's what part of the training was about. In Vietnam, he was a helicopter pilot assigned to Aerial Reconnaissance. "Our job was to find the enemy. The easiest way to find the enemy was to have them shoot at you." He flew UH-1C gunship Hueys which carried mini-guns or rockets as well as two door gunners.

UH–1C Helicopter flown by D. Bressem (Source: Veterans' History Project)

Bressem was awarded a Soldier's Medal and the Purple Heart. The Soldier's Medal is awarded to personnel who has distinguished himself or herself by heroism not involving conflict with an enemy.

In an interview with the Veterans' History Project, when asked if the war in Vietnam was for a "just cause," Bressem replied, "I don't think I can say that. It was never a war that we were going to win." After a mission in which he was trying to root out the enemy and ended up burning down an entire village in the process, Bressem's reaction was:

"Thinking we made more enemies than we killed today."

Bressem later joined the organization, Vietnam Veterans Against the War. He also went to Washington and testified before congress about war crimes.When former President Jimmy Carter received the Nobel Peace Prize in 2002, "for his decades of untiring effort to find peaceful solutions to international conflicts, to advance democracy and human rights, and to promote economic and social development," Dave Bressem recalled what Carter said in his speech accepting the award:

"War is sometimes a necessary evil, but it's always evil."

Day 56, 4 December 1967 – "Blue Ghost"

Tom had the honor of designing and painting the Blue Ghost call sign on most of the C-Model gunship helicopters when they began their stay in Chu Lai. He had originally designed and painted the Blue Ghost while training in Fort Knox, Kentucky.

In talking about the origin of the Blue Ghost call sign, 1967-1968 Blue Ghost Bill Hatch, recalled this story: "It had been decided while at Fort Knox, that C Troop would be known as the Ghost Riders. However, upon arrival in Vietnam, Major Marett, the troop commander, was informed that Ghost Riders was already being used by a helicopter company operating in the central highlands. Since we already had Tom Pueschel's Blue Ghosts, we simply became the Blue Ghosts."

Tom Pueschel painted the Blue Ghost on most of the helicopters in Ky Hai Heliport, Chu Lai

Bllue Ghost patches: 1967 (left), later evolved to 1968 (right)

Day 31 - Day 61, 9 November 1967 – 9 December 1967 – The first Air Medal

This is to certify that the President of the United States of America authorized by Executive Order, May 11, 1942, has awarded
The Air Medal
to
Warrant Officer W1 Thomas R. Pueschel, United States Army for Meritorious Achievement While Participating in Aerial Flight in the Republic of Vietnam during the period 9 November 1967 to 9 December 1967.
Given under my hand in the city of Washington this Eighth day of February 1968.

The Air Medal – 9 November –9 December 1967 (Tom's 1st Air Medal)

Signed: S. W. Koster, Major General, Commanding
Signed: Stanley R. Resor, Secretary of the Army

Tom was awarded The Air Medal for the period 9 November - 9 December 1967. It was the first of many Air Medals. The Air Medal was awarded "for meritorious achievement while participating in aerial flight in support of combat ground forces in the Republic of Vietnam."

During the Vietnam War, the U.S. Army awarded The Air Medal to Warrant Officers or Commissioned pilots and enlisted crew for actual flight time. In the case of helicopter pilots, who were continuously flying hazardous duty–combat assaults and extractions–each mission was recognized as one hour or more of flight time.

The citation for the award states that The Air Medal is presented for meritorious achievement through participation in more than 25 aerial missions over hostile territory.

The Air Medal (left)

Silver Oak Leaf Cluster
(top center)

Gold Oak Leaf Cluster
(top right)

The Air Medals

The first award is the medal as shown. Subsequent awards are Oak Leaf Clusters (OLCs) which are attached to the medal. A bronze Oak Leaf Cluster is for a single additional award – an Air Medal with a bronze cluster would indicate that the recipient has received the award twice – two awards or more than 50 missions in combat assault flights. A silver Oak Leaf Cluster would indicate five additional awards or more than 125 missions in combat assault flights. Four OLCs could be added to the medal and extra ribbons were worn to hold extra OLCs. In 1968, numerals could replace the oak leaf clusters to simplify their display.

Tom received this first medal in February 1968.In addition, Tom would be awarded six (6) Oak Leaf Clusters, for the December 1967 to January 1968 timeframe, when he was logging between two and three missions each day, every day.

By the end of his tour in Vietnam, Tom would be awarded the Air Medal and 35 Oak Leaf Clusters, representing over 900 aerial missions of combat assault flights, an average of over two missions per day, where he "distinguished himself by meritorious achievement, while participating in sustained aerial flight" over hostile territory.

Day 62, 10 December 1967 – "Killing people was never one of my favorite pastimes."

10 December 1967

Dear Mom & Dad,

I received a letter and a package from you today. Thanks for sending the India ink and stuff. I appreciate it.

I'm sorry if I don't write too much, but there really isn't all that much to write about that is worth telling. Most of the time, I end up taking off at dawn and not returning until after dark, and I am usually just a walking zombie by then. Also, every now and then, I have to pull an extra duty such as Officer of the Guard, like I am tonight, and I am beat. I try to catch as much sleep as I can whenever I can, but that usually only adds up to an average of from four to six hours per night, and it is beginning to tell on me. Also, I am now, the armament officer for the weapons platoon, and that makes my day an hour or two longer than everyone else's. Uncle Sam sure is making me earn my keep right now!

A couple days ago, we had a distinguished visitor at our forward camp – old "Westy" himself (General Westmoreland). Your prodigal son is getting up in the world!! I flew gunship cover and escort for him when they took him on a little tour of our area of operation. Also, today we had a visit from some congressman or something from Nebraska. Lately, it seems, we have had more VIP's around here than we know what to do with!!

I think Veda is planning on trying to get up to visit you all sometime around New Year's or so. Please give her a nice warm welcome and put her at ease. I think she is a little nervous about visiting her future in-laws without me along for moral support. She's so afraid that you won't like her, but I know those fears are needless. You'll have to admit, especially when you get to know her better, that if I do not have much of anything else, my taste in women is nothing short of superb, but, of course, I speak from a somewhat prejudiced point of view!!! She's quite a gal, Mom & Dad, and now that I've found her, I honestly don't know what I would do without.

Things are going ok for me around here, all things considered, so don't worry too much about me. It's not as bad over here as everyone seems to think it is. True, it is far from being pleasant, but things could always be a lot worse. We have our trials and tribulations every now and then, and killing people was never was one of my favorite pastimes, but that's the name of the game

71

and we must see this macabre game of chess through to the end, whatever it might be. I am prepared to meet whatever God or man should put before me to meet, and I will deal with the situation, whatever and wherever it may be, to the best of my ability. After that, the outcome is not for me to say, but I think I am stubborn and determined enough to see it through and survive.

I had better run. Take care and may God bless. I miss you all very much!

For this soldier, it was a battle of two wars. There was the physical war in Vietnam in which he was trying his best just to live another day, while still doing what he had to do amidst blood and guts and gunfire and loss. Then there was the mental war when trying to make sense of all he had been taught about how precious human life was, that every life matters, and about the virtues of being good. Yet here Tom was, in this war in the jungle and in the jungle of war, learning how to take lives at an improbable rate, doing his duty as he must, seeking justification, and preparing to deal with consequences. He was in Vietnam because of his sense of duty. He did nothing wrong to end up there. If not me, then who? he thought. He was resolved to doing his duty but recognized that he didn't like playing the "macabre game of chess" that he'd been forced to play. He was "stubborn and determined enough to see it through and survive." Only a short time before, he had been on the deck of the USNS Walker writing this in his October 18 letter home:

"Can I really take the life of a man, and afterwards, can I really justify that act by attributing it to my own instinct for self-preservation? I don't expect you to answer my questions, but it seems to help to 'talk it out' and I know that sometime, somewhere, with God's help, I will find the answers and ease my unquiet soul. It is something I will have to work out for myself."

Maybe there are some answers out there, answers that might ease the "unquiet soul." But in the end, is that even possible?

Day 66, 14 December 1967 – Weekly Casualties of U.S. Troops in Vietnam

During this one week of the Vietnam War, 194 American soldiers were killed. Which left 194 American families grieving. Weekly Casualties reports made the war seem like it was numbers game. The war was not about numbers.

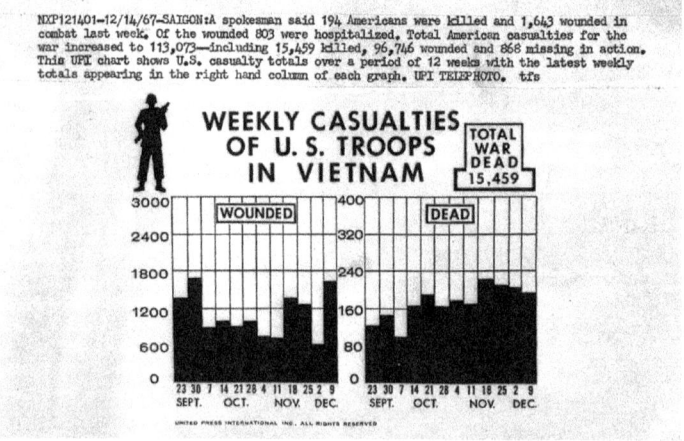

Weekly Casualties Report for week ending 12/14/1967

Casualty Chart for the Vietnam War, 1967

12/14/1967-Saigon, Vietnam - A spokesman said that 194 were killed and 1,643 wounded in combat last week. Of the wounded, 803 were hospitalized. Total American casualties for the war increased to 113,073 – including 15,459 killed, 96,746 wounded and 868 missing in action. (Source: Vietnam Press Photos)

The Joint Chiefs of Staff (JCS) presented this view of the war at the end of 1967:

It was bloody. During 1967, 23,199 allies were killed, and 88,000 enemy were killed.

It was "a year of military progress" with a "definite shift in the military situation favorable to us." Allied forces "had increasingly neutralized enemy base areas." The enemy had been driven to border areas in Laos and Cambodia, sanctuaries for protection, and the population and area under enemy control in South Vietnam had slowly but steadily declined.

As the JCS touted these gains in 1967, they cautioned that the "enemy was not defeated" and was gaining critical knowledge in the deployment of new weaponry. There was worry about large enemy troop build ups and that the enemy was looking for a "spectacular win in South Vietnam in the near future." However, Admiral Sharp countered that through "careful exploitation of the enemy's vulnerability and application of our superior firepower, we should expect our gains of 1967 in South Vietnam to be increased many fold in 1968."

The JCS assessment would prove only partially correct. The year 1968 was often called the "turning point" in the war. The enemy was not defeated. And the soldiers kept fighting.

The Situation at the End of 1967

During 1967, South Vietnamese, FWMAF, and US forces had suffered casualties totaling 23,199 killed in action and 93,791 wounded. According to allied estimates, the enemy during the year had lost more than 88,000 killed. What had been the strategic effect of this bloodletting?[38]

The US commanders in the theater viewed 1967 as a year of military progress in the war. In a typical assessment, Admiral Sharp, summing up operations for the year, reported to the Joint Chiefs of Staff that there was a "definite shift in the military situation favorable to us." He declared that a "significant increase in the strengths and capabilities of allied forces" had facilitated expansion of combat operations to an extent that denied the enemy "the capability to conduct significant operations in the populated areas." Allied ground forces, closely supported by tactical air and ARC LIGHT strikes, had increasingly neutralized enemy base areas, located and destroyed his supplies, and pushed his large units into sparsely populated regions where food was scarce. Most of the enemy main force had been driven to positions near the borders where they took advantage of Laotian and Cambodian sanctuaries for protection and re-supply. Sharp claimed also that steady progress had been made in destroying communist local forces and political infrastructure. As a result, the proportion of the population and area of South Vietnam under enemy control had slowly but steadily declined.

In spite of these favorable trends, Admiral Sharp cautioned, the enemy was not defeated. The North Vietnamese and Viet Cong had "demonstrated a willingness to accept the situation as it exists and continues to attack, harass, and terrorize in many areas . . . ." Enemy artillery, rockets, and mortars had shown a marked increase in both quantity and caliber, and he had shown increasing skill in employing these weapons. Even more disturbing, Sharp reported was evidence of "recent large unit deployments from North Vietnam which indicate that the enemy may be seeking a spectacular win in South Vietnam in the near future." However, CINC-PAC continued, these enemy capabilities were not overpowering. Through "careful exploitation of the enemy's vulnerability and application of our superior fire power and mobility," he concluded, "we should expect our gains of 1967 in South Vietnam to be increased many fold in 1968."[40]

JCS and the War in Vietnam, 1960–1968 Report, p. 102

Day 69, 17 December 1967 – "27 holes and a lot of gray hair"

Tom volunteered to help out in Dak To, where the fighting was brutal and helicopter losses staggering. The battle for Hill 875 continued its violent ways and raged on for days and became one of the costliest battles of the war.

Tom wrote to his good friend, Bill Utley...

17 December 1967

Dear Bill ——

Greetings and salutations and how the hell are you? I received your letter this evening when I got back in from our forward firebase. It was good to hear from you again. Sorry, if I don't write too much, but to put it bluntly, they've been working my ass off lately and I don't have too much time for things like writing, and I do manage to crank a letter out, it's usually to my "better half," of course! By the way, in my address, it's – Americal Division, not American!!

So, the Army went and screwed you! I figured as much – that's about par for the course! I have learned not to believe anything in this man's army until it's actually happening! It is truly amazing how they ever get anything done as screwed up as they are. Keep in there pitching, though – if you bitch loud enough & long enough, maybe you'll get what you want in the end. You can always try Aviation!!!

Hey, if Marge's parents start giving you static, why don't you tell 'em to shove it and elope?!? As far as Veda & I are concerned, we're getting married as soon after I return as humanly possible, and no one better get in the way or they're going to think it's the Israeli conflict all over again with them in the role of the Egyptians!!!

Don't tell me about the sun — I've forgotten what it looks like! It's the rainy season here at Chu Lai and it has been raining for the past ten days without letup! If this keeps up, I'm gonna have webbed feet.

Hmm — was I anywhere near Dak To? Does Hill 875 ring any bells? I came back from there with <u>twenty-seven</u> *(27) holes in my ship and a lot of gray hair, and that was for just one mission. I spent four days up there and logged a total of thirty-two hours of combat assault time, and I still have nightmares about it. A third of the time was at night, and a night combat assault is a special kind of hell. It was like flying into the middle of an explosion in a fireworks factory. My parents & Veda still don't know about that yet. They think I was in Qui Nhon all that time, and I was — getting my ship put back together, but what they don't know won't hurt 'em, & why make them worry. They worry too much already.*

Things have been pretty quiet around here at Chu Lai. We have been operating about 15 miles north of here and have lost only three ships in all the time we have been here and only two casualties – one with a broken leg and the other with a .30 cal bullet in his thigh. Every once in a while we receive fire from a village, and suddenly that village is no longer on the map! I have taken to loading my rocket tubes with Willie Peter only, so you can see we play for keeps! There is supposed to be a battalion of NVA out there somewhere and, according to intelligence reports, they are supposed to hit our forward base with a mortar attack sometime around Christmas. So far, I think we have wiped out about a third of them, so they may think twice about it. Also, every now & then we catch a few gooks sneaking back over into Cambodia or Laos, and the border suddenly moves westward a couple thousand meters or so. I almost got shot down about 800 meters inside Cambodia the other day, and it was touch and go there for awhile, but I made it back across. I'd have been in for a prime chewing-out if I had gone down over there – not so much for being there, but for being caught. Also, some of the higher-ups in division have come up with some screwed up policy for calling and asking permission to return fire when we find a target. My platoon has therefore adopted what we call the "Grease Pencil" method.

If we receive fire, we kill him & mark it down on our windshield with a grease pencil thusly, and then we call & ask permission to fire. If they say no, well, we just rub the grease pencil off as we fly merrily on our way!

I've got to run – it's 2300 now & 0500 sure comes awful early. Take care and have a Happy Christmas. My best to Marge.

P.S. I wrote this to your home address 'cause I figured you'd be home for Christmas vacation by now

P.P.S. I've got 12 confirmed & about a hundred unconfirmed kills so far.That ought to help the population explosion some!!

KILL FOR PEACE
PIECE

* * *

Battle for Dak To: November 3rd to 23rd, 1967

In mid-November 1967, the CO for the C/7/17 told his men that a unit to the west was involved in heavy fighting and was short pilots and copilots. They had been so shot up and there was an imminent need, and any pilot no matter how green or untested would do. The CO asked for volunteers, and Tom raised his hand.

Tom and his unit would be thrust right into the middle of the battle for Hill 875, later known as "The Hill." He would take intense fire for four days and limp back to base, bruised and battered.

The Battle of Dak To in Kon Tum Province was a bad fight, and a very tough way to get oriented to combat. Starting on November 3rd it would last through November 23rd. In those 20 days, the official estimate of U.S. losses amounted to 361 killed and 15 missing, ARVN losses 73 killed and 18 missing, and enemy (PAVN) losses were estimated in the 1,000–2,000 range. The actual counts in Vietnam were often distorted to paint a more favorable view of the battlefield. The Vietnam News Agency and the Associated Press reported that 2,800 US soldiers and 700 ARVN had been killed during the fighting, far higher than the numbers cited as 'official.' It was also reported that helicopters had flown over 2,100 sorties and 40 helicopters were shot down or lost.

The battle for Hill 875 was one of the costliest and most controversial battles of the war. General Charles P. Stone, who took over the 4th Infantry Division after the battle, stated, "I had the damnedest time getting anybody to show me where Hill 875 was. It had absolutely no importance in the war thereafter. None. It had no strategic value...It made no difference... that the enemy held all those mountains along the border because they controlled no people, no resources, no real growing areas, and suffered a horrible malaria rate. Why... go out there and fight them where all the advantages were on their side." Three of the four regiments that had done the fighting were so badly battered that they could only play a minor part in repelling the soon-to-come Tet Offensive

Military analysts have said that the 'Battle of Dak To' accomplished a key enemy objective as US forces began to move out from cities and lowlands. By January 1968, half of all US combat units were operating away from these key areas, which is what the North Vietnamese wanted as they prepared for the Tet Offensive.Tet was directed at major cities in South Vietnam. With US forces protecting the perimeter, an opening to the battles in the cities was created. In its preparation for the Tet Offensive, the VC announced its willingness to honor a seven-day ceasefire during the Tết holiday, for a period running from 27 January through 2 February 1968. The cease fire was a ruse that would allow VC forces to amass and ready themselves for Tet.

The 'Battle of Dak To' was considered a tactical victory for the US/South Vietnamese forces. They had won the numbers game in terms of body counts. But it was a strategic victory for the North Vietnamese forces, specifically designed to set themselves up for the Tet Offensive, which would soon be there.

Cambodia and Laos

Cambodia and Laos were considered neutral during the Vietnam War but both countries were a very big part of the war. This neutrality meant that the United States could not officially send combat troops there, so no bases were established, and, hence, no immediate support troops if a helicopter was shot down. Pilot and crew would be on their own. This supposed "neutrality" had the effect of setting up a veiled no-fly zone for helicopters, which was not always observed. The Ho Chi Minh Trail went from North Vietnam through Laos and Cambodia to South Vietnam.North Vietnamese troops routinely moved weapons and supplies through Cambodia and would use the countries as a staging area for attacks on South Vietnam.

On 4 December 1967, the U.S. Department of State sent a diplomatic note to Prince Sihanouk of Cambodia, pledging that the U.S. would not cross into Cambodia to pursue PAVN/VC force fleeing from South Vietnam, and promising to respect "Cambodian neutrality, sovereignty, independence and territorial integrity." In effect, U.S. Forces could pursue but that pursuit would be stopped short of the border

On 28 December 1967, Prince Sihanouk gave limited permission for U.S. forces to cross from South Vietnam into Cambodia in order to pursue PAVN/VC.

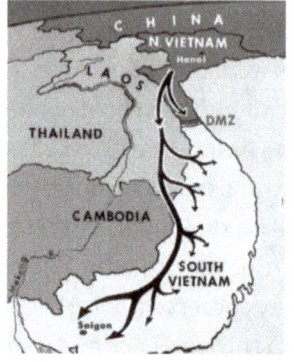 

Ho Chi Minh Trail — through Laos and Cambodia into South Vietnam (left) "Willie Pete" lights up the land (right; source: L. Burrows collection)

"Willie Peter

One of the many horrible weapons of the Vietnam War was White Phosphorus or "Willie Pete." Phosphorus is a highly flammable agent that burns rapidly, releasing white fumes, and is almost impossible to extinguish. In Vietnam, its ostensible use was to mark a target. However, at times, it could be used in the warhead on a rocket. In fact, one of its uses was to set one or more buildings or structures on fire. It combusts on contact with moisture. So, if it landed on skin it became very hot very fast. A real nasty piece of the war business, it is now outlawed by treaty.

"Grease Pencil" Method

The intended use of the grease pencil was putting a mark on the inside of the windshield of a helicopter and using the mark as a sight when firing rockets. Some soldiers came up with other effective uses, including the Grease Pencil Method which spoke to the impossible concept of asking permission before engaging. Kills were marked on the cockpit windshield with a grease pencil.If permission had been granted, the "allowed kill" could be stenciled on the side of the helicopter. If permission wasn't granted, the grease "kill" could simply be erased. There were other ways to deal with the asking for permission, including just maintaining radio silence, then doing what needed to be done, and moving on...no reporting necessary.

Day 74, 20 December 1967 – Bob Hope, Raquel Welch, and Miss World Pay a Visit

"Chu Lai, the Malibu Beach for Losers," cracked Bob Hope as he opened the Christmas Show. "Army, Navy, Air Force, Coast Guard, Seabees, and Marines! Here you have a choice of five wars!" The crowd was huge, camped side by side up the big hill in front of the amphitheater, not an untaken spot. They laughed it up, clapped, and cheered loudly as Bob brought soldiers up from the audience on-stage to give them messages from home. Cameras clicked as Raquel Welch came on stage. She danced and sang—who knew she could sing! Well, she gave it her all and did a pretty good job of it. Besides, her audience didn't care. They just loved looking at her, all decked out in a frilly white top, a mini-skirt and white boots, her legs looking oh so nice.

And don't forget Miss World, Miss Madeleine Hartog Bel of Peru! She was there cracking jokes with Bob and handing out kisses to GIs. Other stars performed, and the troops love it! Smiles all around!

While all around them the earth shook and their world shuddered.

Bob Hope, Raquel Welch, and the Troops at Chu Lai

Bob Hope and company visited eleven U.S. bases in the 1967 tour; Saigon, Long Binh, Bearcat near Bien Hoa, Da Nang, Cu Chi, Pleiku, Lai Khe, Chu Lai, Phu Cat, Phan Rang, and Cam Ranh Bay. From his first USO performance in 1941 to his last during Operation Desert Storm in 1990, Bob Hope would do 57 USO tours, with hundreds of performances. "G.I. Bob" would do nine of his Christmas tours in Vietnam from 1964 to 1972.

Don't Trust a Cease Fire

The Christmas cease-fire began at 1800 hours on the 24th of December and was to last 24 hours through Christmas Day.

Bombing was halted at 1800 hours and resumed right at 1800 the next day, putting the fighting on pause, but not everywhere. There were still incidents and skirmishes occurring in many locations in South Vietnam. This was to be followed by a second cease-fire for the New Year's holiday between December 31 and January 2. That truce would be broken before it even started.

What the North Vietnamese forces did through these truces did not go unnoticed. Intelligence reports including aerial footage showed heavy truck movement (1300 trucks) as the PAVN/VC looked to resupply their forces in the South, all while the cease-fire was going on.

Also, the VC had announced its willingness to observe a seven-day ceasefire during the Tết holiday, for a period running from 27 January through 2 February 1968. This "willingness" wasn't willingness at all, as on 31 January 1968, the VC would begin a coordinated offensive of surprise attacks aimed at breaking the stalemate in Vietnam. It would be known as "The Tet Offensive" and was pivotal in the war in 1968.

Former U.S. President Dwight Eisenhower would later tell President Johnson, "We must not put ourselves in the position of depending upon belief in what a Communist says."

Day 88, 7 January 1968 – "There's enough blood and gore for all"

After Pope Paul VI declared 1 Jan 1968 a 'day of peace', the VC agreed to a 36-hour cease fire for the New Year's Holiday. However, the truce was quickly broken, and fighting intensified.

Tom wrote another letter to his good friend, Bill.

7 January 1968

Dear Bill,

Greetings and salutations from never never land. I say never never because if it had been up to me, I would NEVER have come here in the first place!! However, if you want a noisy and bloody new year, come on over... there's enough blood and gore for all. If I sound kind of bitter, it is probably due to the fact that I am. This place is flat out getting on my nerves. I suppose you heard in the news how our supposed New Year's truce was broken by the other side. Well, that's when it all started in with new fervor and vigor.Since then we have had more than enough to keep us busy twenty-five hours a day. The day after the truce was broken, one of our forward fire bases was attacked around four in the morning with everything but the kitchen sink. When dawn broke, our people had seven wounded and three dead, but also a body count of fifty-

seven (57) dead V.C. just outside the perimeter. A neighboring fire base came out of their little fracas with seventeen wounded and five K.I.A., counting one hundred and sixty-three dead VC outside their perimeter. Yesterday, all our gunships were scrambled at four in the morning (I had just gotten to bed about twelve) because a company of one-hundred and eighty-five (185) ground troops had been over-run about thirty minutes' flight from here. (We made it in twenty.) We couldn't help them much then, because they were in the middle of a valley that was at that time socked in solid with fog from the valley floor on up to the peaks of the surrounding mountains. We did manage to give some support, however, and start air lifting them out the best we could. As soon as the fog lifted a little, we then started our gun runs and poured everything we had in there along with two more platoons of gunships from other units.(We had to make our gun runs from about twenty feet off the deck and break in a climb up through and over the fog.) After we got all of them out of there, the B-52's took over. After that, the artillery pounded it for six hours. Out of those 185 men in that company, there were only forty-three (43) left alive, and of those, all but eight (8) were wounded. The gooks scored a point on that one, but they paid a pretty high price, though we'll never know how high. To top it all off, while we were on our way back here to home plate, we got our first casualty among the gun pilots in my platoon. He was lucky though, for all he got was a face full of plexiglass. Another six inches to the right, and he wouldn't have had any face left at all.(50 cal. Just doesn't leave much of anything when it hits.) They really did a job on our aircraft, though, for out of eleven gunships, we had only two that were flyable this morning, and they worked all night on those.Mine looked a lot more like a hunk of Swiss cheese than a helicopter, and I still don't know how in hell it kept on flying, and I don't want to even ask. It's a wonder *that none of my crew got hit, but I'm not going to ask about that either. I've got enough gray hairs as it is,*

In case you're wondering why I'm typing, it's 'cause my nerves are still a little on the unstable side, and my handwriting is anything but legible.

TOM

The "scores" for this day were 57-3 in one battle and 163-5 in another. And then in yet another battle, in a long day of battles, the *"gooks scored a point on that one"*, with 142 U.S. dead and only 43 left alive, but they *"paid a pretty high price, though we'll never know how high."* Many bodies on the ground. War is Hell. The war rages on...

Day 106, 23 January 1968 – "Pile of unrecognizable ashes."

"The Graves Registration team brought them back in four separate plastic bags, each being about a foot and a half square and about six to eight inches deep."

23 January 1968

Dear Bill — —

Greetings and salutations from this side of a man-made hell. Got your letter a couple days ago, but didn't have time to write a reply till now. I'm not sure I have too much spare time at the moment, but the hell with it. I'm sick and tired of working my "alpha sierra sierra" off to seemingly no avail. The work will still be there when I get back to it, so meanwhile, screw it!!!

We finally got to the wreckage of that gun ship of ours that went down two weeks ago, and recovered what was left of the crew's bodies. It wasn't what you would call a very pleasant experience, for there wasn't too awfully much left, and it had been eleven days since they went down. Most of the wreckage was nothing but a pile of unrecognizable ashes, including the bodies of the crew. In fact, if it hadn't been for a small spring that somehow came through relatively unscathed, we wouldn't have even been able to tell which was the front end of the aircraft. The only part of the aircraft that remained relatively intact was the tail boom assembly, and that was only because it was severed from the main fuselage on impact. I say relatively intact because it had from fifty to sixty .50 and .30 calibre bullet holes running the entire length. It looked more like a piece of metallic swiss cheese rather than a main part of a half million dollar aircraft that it once was. The bodies of the four crew members were mutilated and burned beyond all recognition of human form. The Graves Registration team brought them back in four separate plastic bags, each being about a foot and a half square and about six to eight inches deep. The only way we could identify one of the bodies was by the serial number of the .38 caliber revolver that was still with the body in a position where it must have been strapped. The weapon itself was fused into a solid piece of steel, so you can imagine how hot that fire must have been as the aircraft burned. That is really no great wonder as when they went in, they still had a relatively full load of fuel and had not expended any ordnance. It was an M-5 weapons system, so that means that they had about 300 40mm grenades for the M-5 grenade launcher on board, along with 38 2.75 inch aerial rockets, and the eight white phosphorous grenades we all carry for marking purposes, to say nothing of the ten to twelve regular smoke grenades also carried on board and the 2000 rounds or so of 7.62 ammo for the two door guns. All that, combined with an aircraft skin made of magnesium alloy makes for a loud and very hot fire. All in all, it was a very grisly sight, and not one that I am likely to forget very easily, if at all.

Remind me to tell you sometime about the white refrigerated conexes that are used pretty extensively over here. Those aren't likely to be forgotten easily either.

There is a rumor going around that my troop may soon be OPCON to the 1/1 Cav. which will probably turn out to be pretty good if *it ever comes about. Actually, it is more than just a rumor and it very well may come to be. As it is, we are already in the process of increasing our AO (area of operations) almost all the way up to Da Nang. If that comes about, as it very well will, I don't have to worry about getting enough flight time...I'll be getting more than enough, for we will be covering an area twice as large as the one in which we are presently operating and giving air support to twice as many ground units as we do now. In the past couple of months, my unit, the "Blue Ghosts," has acquired quite a reputation for getting the job done...*

Got to run; take care and stay happy. My best to Marge.

TOM

P.S. Foxtrot Tango Alpha

P.P.S. KILL FOR PIECE!!

The fate of UH1C - tail #66-00745

On January 9, 1968, a mixed team consisting of one LOH (Light Observation Helicopter or "Loach") scout helicopter and one UH-1C gunship helicopter were on a recon mission to see how far the NVA had advanced in an area about 20 miles west of the city of Tam Ky in Quang Tin Province. The gunship-cover crew of the UH-1C (tail #66-00745) consisted of aircraft commander WO1 James L. Phipps, pilot WO Rainier S. Ramos, door gunner SP4 Warren E. Newton, and gunner PFC Fred J. Secrist. It was reported that Fred Secrist was assigned to another crew but wanted to run a mission or two with his buddy, "Fig" Newton. He should not have been aboard when they went out that day. The LOH pilot was LT Don Williamson and he was flying as scout in front of WO Ramos' aircraft.

(left to right) WO James L. Phipps, WO Rainer Ramos, SSG Warren E. Newton, PFC Fred J. Secrist

"Flew right into the side of this mountain."

LT Williamson recalled the mission: "I was the ranking officer and the leader of the mixed team on the 9th. We had been briefed and given an AO (Area of Operations) on the west side of FB (Firebase) Ross and another little outpost just beyond it. They were the last friendly positions and most everything to their west was NVA Country. We called that a 'no fly line' because of the Division support policy." The Americal instructions at the time were not to fly into NVA country because the Division was not in a position to provide extensive support that a downed bird would generate.

LT Williamson continued, "I remember spreading out the maps on some sand bags and we all talked about our route to the AO. Naturally, running a map and flying a LOH low level doesn't make much sense; so I gave my maps to Phipps and Ramos. I still believe we missed a turn and flew west too far (further into NVA country). Anyway, I remember passing over a small pond and receiving fire. I broke and called the Gunship to warn them about the fire. I hadn't even made a complete circle yet when I heard them say that they were taking fire and had been hit. They continued flying on the same heading, so I finished the circle and climbed up behind them. I told them I was 'right on them' so if they needed to land or whatever I was in a position to support them. Anyway, they kept flying straight and flew right into the side of this mountain doing at least 90 knots. We had just refueled and rearmed. Brother, what an explosion and a fire! I made several passes hoping to see someone get out but they really didn't have a chance. On my second pass I was REALLY RECEIVING FIRE. I called for help and remember talking with everyone that evening. They all agreed it was the WORST FIRE they had ever received."

During the first 45 minutes following the crash, the munitions, consisting of 2.75 rockets and 40 mm grenades were exploding every minute or two.

Major Jack Burden at the Hawk Hill FB received LT Williamson's call of a downed aircraft: "When we received Don's call, we launched everything we had (on hand) at Hawk Hill. I was calling back to Chu Lai and coordinating things; but was really desperate to get out there. One ACT (American Combat Team) of the 19th Cav was living at Hawk Hill at the time. They came over and looked at the crash point on the map. They agreed it was certainly bad guy country but said if our troop was going in (meaning putting the Blues on the ground); that they would go as well. At first I really felt good about this and was ready to commit both troops. Finally, I displaced some poor gun pilot and flew out there in Greg Ross's gunship. They must have picked the base camp for a heavy weapons units of an NVA regiment, the fire was really bad! It didn't take long to realize that we would doom both troops if we tried to go in there. Their ship was still burning like mad when I got there, with ammo, especially WPs (white phosphorous) going off. I made a couple of passes at about 50 knots about 20 feet over the site but certainly saw nothing that was encouraging at all. We tried to go back the next day but it was still too hot. There was a small OP (observation post) about 300 meters up the steep hill from the crash site. About a week and a half later, these friendly called us to say that the area was secured. I took a special team in to inspect the site. We found some human remains and the team was pretty positive they had identified four left legs. Even so, they were officially carried as MIA for many years; but I have no doubt that they died."

According to the Department of Defense, "On Jan. 9, 1968, the crew was on a mission over Quang Tin Province (now part of Quang Nam Province), South Vietnam, when the Huey was struck by ground fire, causing it to crash and explode in a North Vietnamese bunker and trench system. The crew was declared missing in action. On Jan. 20, 1968, a U.S. led team recovered the body of Secrist and he was returned to his family for burial."

The other three soldiers were not identified and were classified as MIA. The rule at the time was that if there were no positively identifiable remains, a soldier could not be listed as killed (KIA). This had an alarming effect on the families as the MIA classification gave them hope that their sons were still alive, even though through eye-witness accounts and later inspections of the crash site, it was certain that all four perished in the crash.

The toll on the family of Rainer "Ray" Ramos was especially hard. Ray's mother was German and had lost her first husband and a young daughter in WWII during an Allied bombing raid. After the war ended, she met Ray's father who was a

GI stationed in allied-occupied Germany and Ray was born in Germany in 1947.Some twenty years later, Ray's father died of cancer just weeks before he was to be deployed to Vietnam. As a sole surviving son, he could have opted out of going to Vietnam but out of a sense of duty and commitment to his fellow soldiers, he declined to do that, stayed with his unit, and headed to Vietnam. When Ray was listed as MIA, his mother held out hope and believed he was alive. She would write letters to the military command begging for help in getting Ray home. She had lost two families to the ravages of war and could not let go of the hope of seeing her son again.

The remains of the three MIA soldiers would not be officially identified until 2015 and a memorial ceremony was held on 17 June 2015.

(Source: this account of what happened on January 9, 1968 and the following days was compiled from various sources including the Department of Defense POW/MIA Accounting Agency (DDPA, dpaa.mil), the Defense Visual Information Distributive Service (DVIDS, dvids.net), pownetwrok.org, and The Wall of Faces (VVMF.org) and eye-witness accounts)

Press Release 8 June 2015

"The Department of Defense POW/MIA Accounting Agency (DPAA) announced today that the remains of three servicemen, missing from the Vietnam War, have been identified and will be buried with full military honors.

Army Chief Warrant Officers 3 James L. Phipps of Mattoon, Illinios, and Rainer S. Ramos of Wiesbaden, Germany, were the pilots of a UH-1C Iroquois (Huey) helicopter gunship that was shot down in Quang Tin Province, South Vietnam. Also aboard the aircraft were door gunners Staff Sgt. Warren Newton of

Eugene, Oregon, and Spc. Fred J. Secrist of Eugene, Oregon. The crew was assigned to Troop C, 7th Squadron, 17th Cavalry Regiment, 14th Aviation Group, 1st Aviation Brigade. The crew was buried, as a group, on June 17 at Arlington.

Between August 1993 and August 2011, U.S.-Socialist Republic of Vietnam (S.R.V.) teams surveyed and/or excavated the site three times. From Aug. 6-21, 2011, a joint U.S.-S.R.V. team recovered human remains and personal effects.

In the identification of the recovered remains, scientists from DPAA and the Armed Forces DNA Identification Laboratory (AFDIL) analyzed circumstantial evidence and used forensic identification tools, to include mitochondrial DNA, which matched Secrist's sister and brother. Remains not individually identified represent the entire crew and will be buried as a group."

Ceremony in Arlington Cemetery June 17, 2015 — Top Left "Pershing's Own" marching band; Bottom Left: caisson carrying remains; Right: Black Hawks flyover

Embrace those gentle heroes that you left behind...

To those that did not come back, we honor your service and cherish your memory.

"If you are able, save for them a place inside of you....and save one backward glance when you are leaving for the places they can no longer go.....Be not ashamed to say you loved them....

Take what they have left and what they have taught you with their dying and keep it with your own....And in that time when men decide and feel safe to call the war insane, take one moment to embrace those gentle heroes you left behind...."

This quote was from a letter home by Major Michael Davis O'Donnell who would himself be KIA 24 March 1970 — shot down and killed while attempting to rescue 8 fellow soldiers surrounded by attacking enemy forces. He was posthumously awarded the Distinguished Flying Cross,

James L. Phipps, b. 9 Dec 1943, d. 9 Jan 1968 (age 24 years, 1 month)

Rainer S. Ramos b. 29 May 1947, d. 9 Jan 1968 (age 20 years, 9 months, 11 days)

Warren E. Newton b. 26 March 1949, d. 9 Jan 1968 (age 18 years, 9 months, 14 days)

Fred J. Secrist b. 2 Oct 1948, d. 9 Jan 1968 (age 19 years, 3 months, 7 days)

BLUE GHOST
ALL GAVE SOME, SOME GAVE ALL

James Phipps 1/9/68
Rainer Ramos 1/9/68
Warren Newton 1/9/68
Fred Secrist 1/9/68
Ralph Consavage 3/7/68
Louis Bradley 5/16/68
George Canamare 2/8/69
Jimmy Myers 2/24/69
Richard Watson 6/3/69
Paul Miller 6/3/69
William Martin 7/13/69
Graham Howison 7/13/69
Clifford Weekly 7/13/69
Robert Farrington 12/11/69
Fred Zimpler 2/15/70
James Hardin 2/19/70
James Anella 3/5/70
Elmer Perry 3/5/70
Benito Ponce 3/12/70
Raymond Graver 4/5/70
Myron Berg 4/8/70

4/23/70   Larron Murphy
4/23/70   Dennis Eads
10/14/70   Troy Durden
11/24/70   Samuel Saito
11/30/70   Benjamen Nelson
3/6/71   Daniel Allen
3/6/71   Jerry Flores
3/7/71   Terry McClanahan
3/6/71   Harvey Wright
3/7/71   Mark Afflerbach
3/7/71   Hyrum Port
4/2/72   Ronald Paschall
4/2/72   Byron Kulland
4/2/72   John Frink
6/11/72   Robin Yeakley
6/11/72   James Hackett
6/11/72   Arnold Holm
6/11/72   James Mc Quade
6/11/72   Wayne Bibbs
6/12/72   Richard Wiley

Day 114, 31 January 1968: Tết Offensive

"It was, all in all, a hell of a fight." Blue Ghost pilot John Shephardson on the Tet Offensive.

It was around 4 A.M. on the 31st of January 1968 when the sirens at the Chu Lai Air Base sounded. It started with rockets and mortars. Then sporadic gunfire and more small explosions. And then a fierce ground attack on perimeter defenses. Troops scrambled for cover, grabbing rifles and helmets, and heading for communal bunkers or other places of safety. Hooches were hit, some totally destroyed, hangers and aircraft were on fire. Sandbags piled next to the hooches provided the only defense to the plywood structures. The rockets and mortars kept coming. The ground attack kept coming, too as the enemy attacked from both the south at Dong Binh II and the north at An Tan village. Fire came in from sampans (NVA/VC attack boats) hidden offshore.

Then the sky turned a bright red, on this very dark night. Then the sound. An indescribable sound, reverberating and ringing in our ears. Then fading to a rumble. The shock wave came through along with the sound, a shock wave felt anywhere in the camp. The concussion drove soldiers back against buildings and onto the ground. The force of the explosion knocked down buildings and hangars. Debris rained all over camp.

Vietcong rockets and satchel charges had hit the ammunition dump destroying over 600 tons of bombs and bulk explosives, causing a mushroom cloud of fire and smoke.Huge chunks of shrapnel sprayed everywhere. Explosions and fire, bullets, rockets, and bombs, and smoke everywhere.

Pilots scrambled and had everything in the air by 0500 hours with targets prioritized by HQ. For the next few days, the fighting was fierce and the enemy were often caught out in the open, fighting and dying by the thousands.

It was the start of the **Tết Offensive,** the largest coordinated attack by North Vietnam against the South Vietnam Army and the United States forces and their allies. North Vietnam leaders, military commander General Vo Nguyen Giap, in concert with Ho Chi Minh, authorized the attacks in the thought that they would break and collapse the ARVN forces and bring discontent and rebellion to South Vietnam.

Tết, short for Tết Nguyên Đán is the time for the Spring Festival, and the advent of the Vietnamese Lunar New Year. It is one of the most important holidays in Vietnamese culture. "Festival of the First Morning of the First Day" lasts nine days, and the first day of Tet is the most important. Good fortune on the first day of Tet portended good things to come through the remainder of the year. Hanoi had announced in October that it would observe a seven-day truce from 27 January to 3 February for the Tet holiday, and the South Vietnamese military had made plans to allow recreational leave for approximately half of its forces. The NVA and VC had other intentions.

In 1968, instead of festival and merriment, instead of a time to honor ancestors and attend family reunions, it was the time for war. War and more war. More war than had ever been seen before in Vietnam. The Tet offensive was aimed at breaking a stalemate and it marked with the most hard-fought, bloodiest, and deadliest battles of the war.

"Crack the Sky, Shake the Earth" was the message given to North Vietnamese troops as they were about to embark on this full-out, stand-and-fight offensive. Be ready to fight. Be ready to die.

The fighting would continue well past the nine days of Tet and rage on for months. For Troop C, 7th Squadron, 17th Cavalry (Air), the *Blue Ghosts* would be at it almost every day with little or no let-up for the two months of February and March 1968.

As part of the Americal Division (23rd Infantry), the *Blue Ghosts*, working in concert with the 1st Squadron/1st Cavalry (Armor), would fly in over 200 separate engagements with thousands of sorties. Their AO (Area of Operation) was primarily in the vicinity of the Que Son Valley and the cities of Tam Ky and Hoi An, but they went wherever they were needed. And they were needed a lot and in many places. Both cities and the valley were north of the Chu Lai Air Base. In the Pineapple Forest Battle, the 1/1 and C/7/17 would have one of their greatest victories, killing 180 enemy forces while not losing one of their own number. But, killing was everywhere.

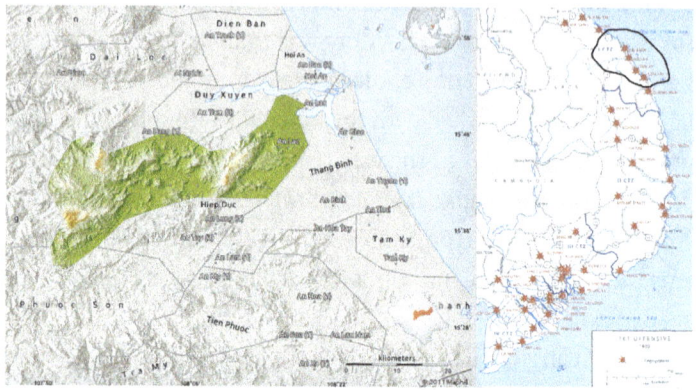

Que Son Valley (left, green); Tet at Chu Lai, Tam Ky, Hoi An, Que Son (right, circled)

Day 123, 9 February 1968 – DFC

It was a long day and a long hard fight, just a week after the Tet Offensive had started.Tet had been one of the few times that the VC/NVA had chosen to stand and fight versus their normal hit-and-run tactics.

For actions performed that day, Warrant Officer Thomas R. Pueschel was awarded the Distinguished Flying Cross (DFC). This was the first time he would be awarded this honor. General Orders #1831 issued 8 April 1968, Award of the Distinguished Flying Cross, are paraphrased here:

For heroism while participating in aerial flight as evidenced by voluntary action above and beyond the call of duty. On Friday the 9th of February 1968, Warrant Officer Pueschel, serving as the pilot-gunner of an armed UH-1C helicopter, provided close air support for a ground unit that was greatly out-numbered and in a severe position. The ground force had depleted its supply of marking smoke, forcing Tom and his crew to make low-level passes to pinpoint enemy positions. With complete disregard for his own safety, he made several gun-runs on the target area while receiving intense hostile fire. On each attack, he maneuvered his aircraft to place maximum effective fire. After moving back to his base

for fuel and ammunition, he continued his attacks until all ordnance was expended. He did this until the enemy broke contact with the infantry unit and retreated. Warrant Officer Pueschel's heroic actions greatly assisted the ground force in repelling the enemy assault. Warrant Officer Pueschel's outstanding flying ability and devotion to duty are in keeping with the highest traditions of the military service and reflect great credit upon himself, the Americal Division, and the United States Army.

Without its colored marking smoke that identified positions on the battlefield, the only way to identify enemy positions was for helicopters to fly low and pinpoint both friendly and enemy positions. As positions were identified, the helicopters attacked.

Fellow pilot John Shephardson who was also awarded a DFC on this same day recalled the events:

"Here's what I remember; this was just a week after the Tet '68 offensive which was the largest enemy action of the entire war. It was the first time (in my experience) that the bad guys chose to stand and fight vs their normal hit-and-run tactics. History has proven that that was a disastrous strategy for them. They lost hundreds of thousands of soldiers and the VC (local guerrillas) were wiped out as a fighting force. We had been pursuing them since Feb 1 as they retreated into their strongholds in the hills.

On the 9th they (NVA or North Vietnamese Army) ran into a US infantry unit acting as a blocking force. This fight was a typical demonstration of the hammer and anvil maneuver which is as old as time. We were part of the hammer, the infantry was the anvil.

The NVA were fighting out of desperation. They knew if they were stopped (trapped) they were done for, so they fought hard.

They overran part of the infantry unit and broke them up into smaller units, dispersed over some area. Because we couldn't know where all the friendlies were, we couldn't employ our usual tactic of just blasting the shit out of a couple of acres and letting someone go in and count the chunks. We needed to be up close and personal on this one, kind of a "don't fire until you see the whites of their eyes" thing which is reflected in Tom's citation.

In my case I spotted an enemy 12.7mm (.51 caliber) anti-aircraft gun and took it out. I think there were a couple of other medals won that day as it was a long, hard fight.

As it turned out I was awarded a second DFC on Mar 4 in almost the same area when (deja vu) the NVA overran a US unit and I got shot down escorting a medevac in.

I'm guessing Tom got his Purple Heart in a cleanup of this fight.

To me, winning 2 medals in 30 days in actions about 500 meters apart tells the story of the whole war – they didn't want to occupy ground and we didn't have enough people to do so and as a result the same ground was won and lost multiple times over the years."

(Note: The hammer and anvil is a military tactic involving the use of two primary forces, one to pin down an enemy, and the other to smash or defeat the opponent with an encirclement maneuver. Source: Wikipedia)

In the following photo, Tom (4th from left) is receiving the DFC award, presented by Troop Commander, Major Jack Eastwood. Standing near Tom are two of his classmates – Fred Nicely to his left and Terry Rippy to Fred's rear. Also receiving a DFC was John Shephardson (not pictured).

WO Thomas Pueschel receiving the DFC for actions on 9 February 1968

An award of the DFC puts its recipients in elite company. Former recipients include former President George H. W. Bush, Senator John S. McCain, numerous astronauts including John Glenn, Buzz Aldrin, and Mark Kelly, and civilians Amelia Earhardt, and Wilbur and Orville Wright. (Note that the DFC is presently limited to military personnel by an Executive Order.)

DFC Medal (left); DFC Certification (right) – 9 February 1968

June 11, 1968

T. R. Pueschel, Now In Vietnam, Awarded Distinguished Flying Cross

Thomas R. Pueschel, son of Mr. and Mrs. Richard Pueschel of 119 Westfield Rd., has been awarded the Distinguished Flying Cross for service in Vietnam.

Pueschel is a 1963 graduate of Holyoke High School, and attended Holyoke Community College and Valparaiso College, each for a period of one year. He enlisted in the Army in 1966, and attended the Army's Primary Helicopter School, Fort Walters, Texas, and its Aviation School at Fort Rucker, Alabama. He received his wings and was commissioned a Warrant Officer in March, 1967. Pueschel has been serving in Vietnam since October, 1967.

The citation indicates that Pueschel distinguished himself "by voluntary action above and beyond the call of duty."

Thomas R. Pueschel

Excerpt from Holyoke (MA) Transcript newspaper – 11 June 1968

Day 129, 15 February 1968: Battlefield Art

The war continues its brutality...and a soldier looks for solace in art. Drawings by Tom Pueschel a.k.a. *"Puesch."*

Note that the soldier in the "Sentinel in the Night" almost looks like a self-portrait.

"Chu Lai, Viet Nam" by 'Puesch' – February 1968

"Sentinel in the Night" by 'Puesch' – February 1968

Day 141, 27 February 1968 – Cronkite: "We are mired in a stalemate."

It was February 27, 1968. Iconic anchorman Walter Cronkite had just returned from a two-week fact-finding trip to Vietnam. His purpose was to see Vietnam firsthand and report on the impact of the month-old Tet Offensive. At 10 P.M. Eastern time, CBS News aired a half-hour news segment, titled, "Report from Vietnam: Who, What, When, Where, Why?" Towards the end of that airing, Walter Cronkite, the "most trusted man in America," delivered the following personal commentary:

"Tonight, back in more familiar surroundings in New York, we'd like to sum up our findings in Vietnam, an analysis that must be speculative, personal, subjective.

Who won and who lost in the great Tet offensive against the cities? I'm not sure. The Viet Cong did not win by a knockout, but neither did we. The referees of history may make it a draw. Another standoff may be coming in the big battles expected south of the Demilitarized Zone. Khe Sanh could well fall, with a terrible loss in American lives, prestige and morale, and this is a tragedy of our stubbornness there; but the bastion no longer is a key to the rest of the northern regions, and it is doubtful that the American forces can be defeated across the breadth of the DMZ with any substantial loss of ground. Another standoff.

On the political front, past performance gives no confidence that the Vietnamese government can cope with its problems, now compounded by the attack on the cities. It may not fall, it may hold on, but it probably won't show the dynamic qualities demanded of this young nation. Another standoff.

We have been too often disappointed by the optimism of the American leaders, both in Vietnam and Washington, to have faith any longer in the silver linings they find in the darkest clouds. They may be right that Hanoi's winter-spring offensive has been forced by the Communist realization that they could not win the longer war of attrition, and that the Communists hope that any success in the offensive will improve their position for eventual negotiations. It would improve their position, and it would also require our realization, that we should have had all along, that any negotiations must be that — negotiations, not the dictation of peace terms.

For it seems now more certain than ever that the bloody experience of Vietnam is to end in a stalemate. This summer's almost certain standoff will either end in real give-and-take negotiations or terrible escalation; and for every means we have to escalate, the enemy can match us, and that applies to invasion of the North, the use of nuclear weapons, or the mere commitment of one hundred, or two hundred, or three hundred thousand more American troops to the battle. And with each escalation, the world comes closer to the brink of cosmic disaster.

To say that we are closer to victory today is to believe, in the face of the evidence, the optimists who have been wrong in the past. To suggest we are on the edge of defeat is to yield to unreasonable pessimism. To say that we are mired in stalemate seems the only realistic, yet unsatisfactory, conclusion.

On the off chance that military and political analysts are right, in the next few months we must test the enemy's intentions, in case this is indeed his last big gasp before negotiations. But it is increasingly clear to this reporter that the only rational way out then will be to negotiate, not as victors, but as honorable people who lived up to their pledge to defend democracy and did the best they could.

This is Walter Cronkite. Good night."

Walter Cronkite's words were heard across America. *"To say that we are mired in stalemate seems the only realistic, yet unsatisfactory, conclusion."* He had called the Vietnam war unwinnable with the *"only rational way out then will be to negotiate, not as victors, but as an honorable people who lived up to their pledge to defend democracy and did the best they could."*

It was a turning point in public support for the war. Walter Cronkite, as had most journalists, had initially been a supporter of the Vietnam war effort, but this trip had changed him. As support for the war plummeted drastically following the broadcast, President Lyndon Johnson was reported to have said, *"If I've lost Cronkite, I've lost Middle America."* Just weeks later, President Johnson announced that he would not seek re-election for president.

Day 144, 1 March 1968 – "Literally shooting them to pieces."

The combat hours kept piling up. And three-day rest periods don't last three days. The Battle of Tam Ky would begin on March 3 and last through March 6 and it would be another hell fight.

"1 March 1968

Dear Bill,

Greetings and salutations from the ass-hole of the world – Viet Nam, 'cause if God wanted to give the world an enema, he'd shove it in here!

Things have been sort of popping around here — there was supposed to be a battalion of NVA back here in the foothills somewhere, assembling for a second wave attack on Chu Lai and Tam Ky, and for the past week, we have been literally shooting them to pieces. I kind of doubt that there'll be any attack for quite some time now, 'cause according to G-2 reports, we clobbered about 70% of their force, and we're still picking up stragglers here and there. It was like an old fashioned turkey shoot. Now, they're giving me a three-day rest period 'cause I flew more than 140 combat hours last month, and God only knows I can use it.

Well, a unit of the 82nd Airborne moved in here not too long ago, *and boy, have they got a lot to learn. They came with the attitude that they were going to take over the place and now are sort of ticked off 'cause we promptly put them in their place. So now, like a bunch of spoiled brats, they are striking back with smoke grenades in our shower, and a couple of them even took potshots at our helicopter as we flew by. Well, a smoke grenade is one thing we retaliate with CS, but shooting at our aircraft — I didn't give a shit who it is, he shoots at me, I shoot back with everything I've got handy. My CO has now informed them that any repetition of this, and we will take them under fire with every gun-ship we have, and we're pretty good at our job — we've had enough practice. Those two GIs will be paying for the damage they did to our chopper for quite some time, to the tune of $20,000, and on E-2 pay, it's going to take a while. (They were buck sergeants at one time.) It's bad enough that we have to fight the gooks, so that we strongly object to taking any bullshit from a branch of pin-heads who haven't even seen combat yet! From the looks of them, though, when they do meet Charlie, they're going to get their asses kicked, hard.*

Got to run. Take care and stay happy.

Day 149, 6 March 1968 – "Purple Hearts were common, unfortunately."

"Purple hearts were common, unfortunately. We had a lot of wounds." A soldier's lament about the Battle of Tam Ky. That's the story of the Vietnam War.

The Battle of Tam Ky began on March 3 and lasted through March 6. It began with heavy mortar and rocket fire on Hawk Hill, the firebase just a few miles from Chu Lai Air Base. US forces were composed of the 1st squad/1st cavalry/23rd infantry, which included 3 armored cavalry units, plus an air cavalry troop— the *Blue Ghosts* (C/7/17). Following the mortar and rocket attack, the Blue Ghosts discovered the rocket-firing positions on Hill 34 to the west of base camp. The field of battle expanded. Fighters were brought in but much of the battle was fought with armored vehicles and ground forces, supported with helicopters.

The result was an overwhelming US victory with 436 NV soldiers killed and many weapons captured. The 3rd NV Regiment was decimated and ceased to exist as an effective fighting force.

Tom was wounded on the last day of the battle, as the *Blue Ghosts* were performing clean-up actions in this fight. His helicopter received heavy fire and a piece of shrapnel ended up lodged in Tom's left leg. Tom would be patched up in a field hospital, given a little rest, and then go back to it again. He had earned the Purple Heart.

"The United States of America, To All who shall see these Presents, Greeting: This is to certify that the President of the United States of America has awarded the Purple Heart, established by General George Washington, at Newburgh, New York, August 7, 1782, to Warrant Officer W1 Thomas R. Pueschel, United States Army, For Wounds Received in Action, in the Republic of Vietnam on 6 March 1968, given under my hand in the city of Washington, This Twenty-fifth Day of April 1968." Signed S.W. Koster, Major General, USA Commanding, and Stanley R. Resor, Secretary of the Army.

Day 159, 16 March 1968 – My Lai massacre and cover-up

This short description of the My Lai massacre is included for its historical context. My Lai was a small village, a sub-division of Son My village, and was located just a short thirty miles from Chu Lai Air Base. A helicopter pilot (Hugh Thompson) intervened during the massacre. The killing was stopped. An Americal Infantry Division was involved.

On March 16, 1968, a platoon of American soldiers brutally killed as many as 500 unarmed civilians at My Lai, one of a cluster of small villages located near the northern coast of South Vietnam. The crime, which was kept secret for nearly two years, later became known as the My Lai Massacre.

The Mỹ Lai massacre was the mass murder of unarmed South Vietnamese civilians by U.S. troops in Son Tinh District, South Vietnam, on 16 March 1968. Between 347 and 504 unarmed people were killed by the U.S. Army soldiers from Company C, 1st Battalion, 20th Infantry Regiment and Company B, 4th Battalion, 3rd Infantry, 11th Brigade 23rd (Americal) Infantry Division. Victims included men, women, children, and infants. Some of the women were gang-raped and their bodies mutilated, and some mutilated and raped children who were as young as 12. Twenty-six soldiers were charged with criminal offenses, but only Lieutenant William Calley Jr., a platoon leader in C Company, was convicted. Found guilty of murdering 22 villagers, he was originally given a life sentence, but served three-and-a-half years under house arrest after President Richard Nixon commuted his sentence.

The Sơn Mỹ Memorial is a memorial to victims of the My Lai Massacre in Son My, Vietnam. This monument was sculpted and donated by Vietnamese artist Ho Thu, husband of Vo Thi Lien who was one of the few survivors of this atrocity. She was only 13 years old at the time. (sources: excerpted from PBS, Wikipedia, The New Yorker)

Son My Memorial, built in 1978 in memory of the victims of the My Lai Massacre

Day 166, 23 March 1968 – "To Dance is To Live"

Two hundred more days and that'll make a year. Two Hundred Days to go. And "To dance is to live."

23 March 1968

Dear Mom & Dad,

Greetings and salutations from your prodigal son in Southeast Asia! Got a package from Aunt Margaret today – would you thank her for me? I haven't got too much time for writing letters right now and will probably not be able to write and thank her myself for quite some time.

Only two hundred days to go and I will be able to bid this place farewell for good (I hope), and I sure am looking forward to that day! I only hope the days to follow will pass quickly for I have been away much too long already and I long to leave this bloodshed and fighting behind me.

One of my buddies made a remark the other day – he saw the picture that Veda and I had taken together just before I left, and he commented that I looked much younger in the picture than I do now. Personally, I have not noticed any drastic change in my appearance, but evidently it just isn't apparent to me for he is not the only one who seems to think I have aged quite a bit in the past

six months. I wonder what it's going to be like after a whole year!
I've got to run. ——- Take care and may God bless ——-

Day 170, 27 March 1968 – "Every Guest a V.I.P!"

After the battles of Dak To, Hoi An, Tam Ky, and Tet, Tom got a little chance to recuperate. If just momentarily, he was able to forget the ever constant pressure of battle...forget bullet holes, rockets, mortars. Tom had earned some time at the R & R Center, Camp Zama, Japan, where *"Every Guest a V.I.P.!"*

 **R & R CENTER**
Camp Zama, Japan

"27 March 1968

Dear Mom & Dad,

Greetings and salutations from Tokyo, Japan! I just arrived not too long ago, and already I kind of like it here. (That's probably largely due to the fact that it's not Viet Nam, but we won't go into that, ok?)

They've got quite a few package tours available which promise to keep you quite busy for the duration of our stay, and I think I just might take one as I doubt if I will get anywhere and see as much by myself.Besides, I might even get to go skiing in Nikon, which I wouldn't mind a bit. One thing that's going to be hard to adjust to is the difference in temperature – compared to Viet Nam, this place is downright cold! I hate to imagine what it's going yo be like when I come back home in the middle of October!

Oops! Running out of paper, I'll say so long and send a postcard when I get a chance.

`Every Guest a V. I. P. "

Love,
Den

Not exactly a vacation at some swanky joint but it was the only thing available. Seven days off then back to the battlefield. This was what soldiers had to do.

Day 114-Day 174, 31 January 1968 – 31 March 1968: Tết Offensive; Presidential Unit Citation

The Army ***Presidential Unit Citation (PUC) for Extraordinary Heroism*** was awarded to the 1st Squadron. 1st Cavalry and to the *Blue Ghosts* of Troop C, 7th Squadron, 17th Cavalry (Air). It is awarded to units that display gallantry that set them apart from other units and who demonstrate exceptional heroism in action against an armed enemy. The official citation was awarded and signed by President Nixon on 26 August 1969. (Excerpted from history.com)

THE PRESIDENTIAL UNIT CITATION
FOR EXTRAORDINARY HEROISM
TO THE
1ST SQUADRON, 1ST CAVALRY (ARMOR) AND
TROOP C, 7TH SQUADRON, 17TH CAVALRY (AIR)
UNITED STATES ARMY

The 1ST SQUADRON, 1ST CAVALRY (Armor) and C TROOP, 7TH SQUADRON, 17TH CAVALRY (AIR), of the Americal (23rd Infantry) Division distinguished themselves by extraordinary heroism while engaged in military operations against hostile forces in the Republic of Vietnam from 31 January to 31 March 1968.

During this period these units sought out and encountered heavily armed, well-supplied, and aggressive North Vietnamese and Viet Cong forces of company, battalion and regimental size in more than 217 separate engagements in the southern I Corps tactical area in the vicinity of Tam Ky and Hoi An. Opposing a highly motivated enemy that consistently occupied heavily fortified bunkers and tunnel complexes with excellent fields of fire, the 1/1 Cav supported by C/7/17 Cav, displayed exceptional professional ability, efficient teamwork, personal initiative, driving aggressiveness and dauntless courage in repeatedly defeating the enemy. Operating independently, with attached infantry, or in conjunction with Republic of Vietnam forces, the 1/1 Cav supported by C/7/17/Cav, employed rapid movement, tenacious pursuit, and violent assault to defeat the enemy, killing 1,046 North Vietnamese and Viet Cong while sustaining only 11 fatal casualties of their own.

Through their magnificent efforts, the 1/1 Cav supported by C/7/17 Cav, added materially to the successes attained by the Americal Division on the field of battle. The conspicuous gallantry and extraordinary heroism displayed by all members of both units are in keeping with the highest traditions of the military services and reflect great credit on them, the Americal Division and the United States Army.

No medal is awarded for the Presidential Unit Citation. The Army presents the citation to each individual in the unit with a blue ribbon with a gold trim border.

131

As stated in the PUC, the unit "operating independently, ... employed rapid movement, tenacious pursuit, and violent assault to defeat the enemy, killing 1,046 North Vietnamese and Viet Cong while sustaining only 11 fatal casualties."

Fellow pilot and good friend to Tom, John Shephardson, gave the following account of the battles that the Blue Ghosts faced in February and March of 1968. In addition to the PUC, Shephardson would individually be awarded two Distinguished Flying Crosses (DFCs) for "heroism while participating in aerial flight" during this time period.

John Shephardson

John Shephardson: *"The period starting with Tet on Jan 29 1968 and continuing through the period cited in the PUC (31 March 1968) was one of the most intense combat in I corps (thats "eye, not 1), the northern military region of South Vietnam. The bad guys thought the Tet Offensive would end the war. When it didn't they reverted to a second strategy of trying to cut off the area from the Que Son Valley north to the DMZ from RVN (Republic of Vietnam) control. As a result while fighting died way off in most of the country following the failed Tet Offensive it continued at a very high level in our area. It seemed that the bad guys thought that if they could take the city of Tam Ky and cut off the main north-south highway they could achieve the secondary goal. They moved major units into our area to replace their Tet losses. The end result was that for two months we could and did engage in major confrontations every day. The enemy used an area we referred to as Cigar Island as a base. It's an area that fronts on the ocean but is cut off from the mainland by waterways on its southern and western side and by the river just south of Hoi An. It seemed their theory was that we couldn't get tanks and ACAVs (Armored Cavalry Assault Vehicles) on and off that island. They were very wrong. I think they also miscalculated the difficulty of moving their weapons and ammo on and off the island. We were able to cut off their supply routes (primarily by ocean) and to roll over base areas almost at will. Truth is it was kind of a turkey shoot. They had no chance. At the same time there were multiple battles near Tam Ky, along Route 1 and in the Que Son valley itself (their route overland from Laos) and they lost every one. The 2nd NVA division along with supporting regiments was apparently removed from the order of battle because it was decimated. I thought at the time that if we had pursued the remnants of their forces back into Laos we could have stamped them out. Turns out most historians agree it was a botched opportunity. But I was a Warrant Officer, not a General so we didn't pursue.*

As you can imagine from the PUC there were lots and lots of bodies left on the field by the enemy. As I remember it some were still visible late in the tour. It was, all in all, a hell of a fight."

The Tet Offensive would end with the VC and the NVA suffering catastrophic losses to their forces. The sheer brutality of the fighting, shown nightly on television sets across the United States, would contribute to the erosion of public support at home and served as a turning point in the war.

The fighting was constant and brutal. At times, the soldiers were merciless.

Day 175, 1 April 1968 – C becomes F

On the 1st of April 1968, the "*Blue Ghosts*" of C Troop were officially redesignated F Troop, 8th Cavalry. Under this name, the troop served in Vietnam until 26 February 1973. The *Blue Ghosts* were made up of about 160 men and 26 helicopters.

Day 178, 4 April 1968 – "As far as the hold on the bombing goes, it remains to be seen."

The President called for a partial halt in the bombing of North Vietnam. Soldiers on the ground feared the impact of that decision.

4 April 1968

Dear Mom & Dad —

Just a few lines to say hello and to let you know that I am now back at the business of waging war. Before I go any further, the Army went and changed my address again. It is as follows:

WO Thomas R. Pueschel, W3———,

F Troop, 8th Cavalry, Americal Division

APO San Francisco 96325

As far as Capt' Fournier goes, I haven't been able to get in touch with him yet, but probably will within the next few days. He's the S-3 of the 14th Battalion here at Chu Lai, and before we changed to F Troop, 8th Cav., my unit was attached to the 14th Ba. From what they tell me in operations, I guess he has been trying to get a hold of me also, but so far, each time one of us tries, the other is usually off somewhere else. I've got the day after tomorrow off, so

I should be able to reach him then, OK?

Things have been pretty quiet around here lately, and as far as the hold on the bombing goes, well, it remains to be seen, I guess, but meanwhile, the enemy will have an easier time supplying its troops, and if no peace is made, (which I seriously doubt will happen) then they will be able to hit us all that much harder, and I don't care one iota for the idea!!! Personally, I think stepping up the bombing might have helped more than stopping it. If the enemy has enough time to build up their bases, we could very well lose our freedom of the skies over here, and I don't particularly relish the thought of tangling with a Mig with my helicopter. It would be one-sided dog fight with all the odds in his favor.

I've got to run — I'm OD tonight and there's no rest for the weary. Take care and may God bless. Stay happy!

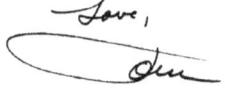

On 31 March 1968, in a nationally televised speech to the nation, President Lyndon B. Johnson announced a partial halt of bombing missions over North Vietnam and proposed initiating peace talks. In his speech, the President emphasized the need for both sides to immediately begin negotiations over the war. It was a bold attempt to get peace talks started, and with the NVA's devastating losses during Tet, there was thought that they might be willing to participate.

"There is no need to delay the talks that could bring an end to this long and this bloody war. Tonight, I renew the offer I made last August—to stop the bombardment of North Vietnam. We ask that

talks begin promptly, that they be serious talks on the substance of peace. We assume that during those talks Hanoi will not take advantage of our restraint. We are prepared to move immediately toward peace through negotiations.

So, tonight, **in the hope that this action will lead to early talks, I am taking the first step to de-escalate the conflict.** *We are reducing, substantially reducing, the present level of hostilities. And we are doing so unilaterally, and* **at once.**"

Towards the end of the speech, President Johnson announced his intention not to run for another term in office, leaving the door open for other candidates including anti-war candidate Eugene McCarthy, rising star Bobby Kennedy, and then Vice-President Hubert Humphrey:

"With America's sons in the fields far away, with America's future under challenge right here at home, with our hopes and the world's hopes for peace in the balance every day, I do not believe that I should devote an hour or a day of my time to any personal partisan causes or to any duties other than the awesome duties of this office—the Presidency of your country. **Accordingly, I shall not seek, and I will not accept, the nomination of my party for another term as your President.**"

The New York Times

LATE CITY EDITION

JOHNSON SAYS HE WON'T RUN; HALTS NORTH VIETNAM RAIDS; BIDS HANOI JOIN PEACE MOVES

ROCKEFELLER URGES ALBANY LEADERS TO SPEED BUDGET

Liberals Designate Javits; Nickerson Race Confused

TAX RISE PUSHED

DMZ IS EXEMPTED

Increase in War Costs; Johnson Sets No Time Cited—No Specific Cuts Suggested

Limit on Halting of Air and Sea Blows

SURPRISE DECISION

President Steps Aside in Unity Bid—Says 'House' Is Divided

3 Beachfront Hotels Destroyed by Fire In Rockaway Park

HOUSE PLAN SPURS INVESTING ABROAD

Kennedy Sets News Parley

Political Chiefs Stunned;

NEW YORK, MONDAY, APRIL 1, 1968

10 CENTS

Day 180, 6 April 1968 – "Done got my promotion tonight."

CW2 Thomas R. Pueschel. Congratulations!

6 April 1968

Dear Mom & Dad —

I haven't got too much time, but I just thought I'd write and let you know that from now on you can address all future mail to me as CW2 Pueschel – ok? I done got my promotion tonight! That extra pay is going to help too, especially after Veda and I get married.I figured it out and I'll be making almost $8000.⁰⁰ per year. I think we should be able to get by on that, don't you?!?

Got to run —- take care and may God bless ———

Love,
Om

Warrant Officers are eligible for promotions based on perfor-mance and time served in each rank. There are five grades of Warrant Officers – Warrant Officer 1 (WO1), Chief Warrant

Officer 2 (CW2), Chief Warrant Officer 3 (CW3), Chief Warrant Officer 4 (CW4), and Chief Warrant Officer 5 (CW5).

Warrant Officers are in a hierarchical layer between Non-Commissioned and Commissioned Officers. They are trained in a technical field (e.g., helicopter pilots) and are a key component of the military. Though outranked by commissioned officers, WOs are highly relied upon and respected for their technical and leadership capabilities.

WO Insignia, called the "Eagle Rising"; CW2 Bars (center)

Day 189, 15 April 1968 – "No such thing as a holiday over here."

15 April 1968

Dear Mom & Dad —

Greetings and salutations once again from your prodigal son in Viet Nam! Things are fine with me, though somewhat hectic right now, but I'm kind of used to that by now.

I hope Easter was a nice one —– mine was just like any other day, but I guess that's to be expected, for there is no such thing as a holiday over here.

I seem to remember your asking me how long my R & R was — seven days, not counting travel time —– just enough to unwind a little and come back, but it was darn good to get away from here, even for just a little while.Oh, well, only 177 more days to go, and maybe I won't ever have to come back here again! I sure am looking forward to going home, but it still seems like an awfully long time yet to go.

I still haven't been able to contact Captain Fournier, but that's mainly 'cause I've been flying most every day since I got back and simply haven't had time. Seeing as how he is assigned to the S-3 at 14th Battalion, that means he lives just on the other side of the base here at Chu Lai, but with the way my schedule has been running lately, it might as well be a hundred miles. I promise I'll give him a call first chance — ok?

So what do you think of me being a Chief Warrant Officer anyway? I doubt if I'll get any more promotions while I'm in the Army though, for it takes about seven years in grade to make CW3, and I plan on being a civilian, come 13 March 1970. CW2 is all right, though — sort of in the middle and I can't kick about the pay raise. It's going to help out in the not too distant future.

I've got to run —- take care, stay happy, and may God bless —-

Love,
Denny

Day 193, 19 April 1968 – "It's what you might call a sort of professional tan."

Far, far, far away from Misquamicut Beach in Rhode Island, where we went as kids...

19 April 1968

Dear Mom & Dad —

Well, the Army went and did it again — as of today, my APO number has changed back again to 96374. I wonder how many more times they're going to change my mailing address before this tour over here is over. It's getting downright ridiculous!

Things have been pretty quiet in this neck of the woods — perhaps too quiet. We're all kind of sitting on edge, waiting for something to happen soon — when it does, it'll probably with a loud, resounding bang! Oh, well, at least we are kind of enjoying this little lull — as you know, we have the Pacific Ocean practically at our back door here in Chu Lai and we have kind of cleaned up the beach a little, and it makes a darn nice place to spend your time off, when you get it, and you know how I love the ocean. I'm getting pretty brown being exposed to the tropical sun everyday, but it's what you might call a sort of professional tan for I'm still kind of white under my shirt. I'll have to start lying on the beach during my time off and fix that, I guess. Now that the dry season is here, it hardly ever rains, so we've got plenty of sunshine. I imagine after all this heat, I'll probably freeze to death once I return home — it's not exactly warm in October back there!

I still haven't been able to get in contact with Captain Fournier mainly 'cause so far I haven't had any time off which corresponded to his.One of these days, though — ok? I've got to run — take care, stay happy, and may God bless.

Love,
Jim

Beach at Chu Lai, circa 1968

Day 194, 20 April 1968 – "Most of all, stay a civilian."

A soldier, many miles from home, thinks about his car, and tells his younger brother, Kenny, *"Stay a civilian."*

20 April 1968

Dear Kenny —

How would you like to do me a favor during some of your spare time this summer? I know you like to fool around with cars, so I was wondering if you would perhaps condescend to putting a tachometer in my Corvair? I imagine there is a little extra money in my checking account, so you can get the money for it from Dad – ok? If you can get one that fits into the slot in the dashboard where the clock is supposed to be, so much the better — if not, go ahead and use your own judgment.Also, if you care to and have the time, that car of mine could also use some gauges to replace the "idiot lights" it has now. It's up to you, however — I'll appreciate it very much, but will understand if you don't want to do it. I imagine you'll be spending a lot of your time puttering around with your own car, much less starting to fool around with mine. How do you like your new car, by the way? I'll bet it's a pretty snazzy piece of machinery. Phooy on you – I've got a helicopter – let's see you beat that!!!

Things haven't been too bad around here lately although yesterday we had LOH (scout helicopter) shot down. It had about twenty to thirty holes in it – "gook" who shot at him must have known what he was doing 'cause he stitched him right down the middle with about 6 to 8 inches between bullet holes. However, that "gook" was also very sorry shortly thereafter for being so quick on the trigger — I put a rocket right between his legs and blew him to hell and gone again. As for the crew of the aircraft, the pilot was the only one hit, and that was one round in the leg just above the knee. It bled a lot and probably hurt like hell, but he'll be all right, and in a way, he's kind of happy 'cause it's just bad enough to send him home. It's still a lousy way to go home, though, any way you look at it! Me – I'm just a chicken at heart and prefer going home in one piece – the sight of blood sickens me, especially when it's my own!

I've got to get going – take care and stay happy, and, most of all, stay a civilian!

σ

Day 202, 28 April 1968 – "All joys, unendingly; all pain unendingly."

With 202 days in the wonderland known as Vietnam, Tom took a few moments to reflect on his favorite poem, written by German poet, Johann Wolfgang von Goethe (1749-1832). He had seen many bad things since he arrived in Vietnam. But he remembered the many good things that he had experienced in life. He reflected on the pain and sorrow confronting him every day and the contrast to happier times passed by. He has come to appreciate life much more.

28 April 1968

Dear Mom & Dad ——-

Greetings and salutations from your prodigal son in never, never land! I'm sorry I haven't written in so long, but even though the V.C. haven't been keeping us very busy, the army certainly has.

I guess I should have included a translation along with that poem by Goethe, but better late than never, I guess. Still, I think it sounds much better in German than in English, but the following is roughly the English version of what the poem means to me:

'All is given by the gods,
   the immortal ones,
   to those whom they love —-
   they withhold nothing:
   All joys, unendingly,
   All pain, unendingly ——
   they withhold nothing'

The more I experience the many varied facets of life, the more the words of this poem seem to ring so very true, not only here, in Viet Nam, where pain and sorrow are a more apparent factor in day to day life, and where death whispers in your ear almost instantly, but in more peaceful and more pleasant places remembered from happier times that have already passed by or are looked forward to when this is over."...They withhold nothing... all joys, unendingly, all pain, unendingly..." how true that is and always shall be, but that is the stuff of which comprises life, is it not? When I first came in contact with these words of Goethe, I liked them and found some meaning in them, but not so much as now, for I now have a more intimate knowledge and understanding of both the wonderful and the terrible sides of the street of life, and have come to appreciate many things much more that I once took for granted. Who knows, perhaps I am finally growing up!

I received your letter mentioning Jean's meeting with Dave Bressem and was overjoyed at the news. He's quite a guy, and I'm happy to learn that he's gonna be ok both physically and mentally. If possible, I'd kind of like to hear from him someday if he cares to write, so if he does come to visit you sometime, please either give him my address or send me his, ok?

I've got to be running ——- take care and may God bless ———-

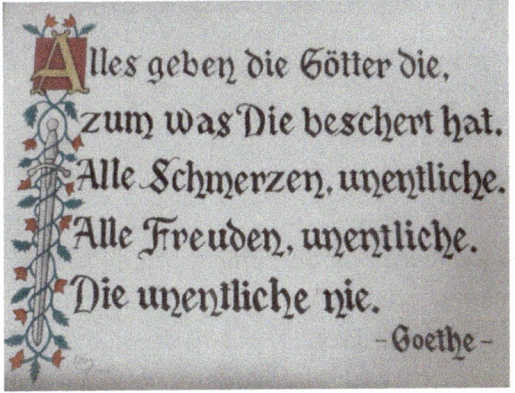

Tom liked this poem so much that he did it in calligraphy. His talent as a calligrapher is on full display.

Day 205, 1 May 1968 – "23 sounds like a nice age to stay for a while."

Happy 23rd Birthday! May 3, 1968.

1 May 1968

   Dear Mom & Dad ——-

   Thank you muchly for the birthday cards – had forgotten all about that fateful day. Also received a card from Uncle Walter & Aunt Esther with a $5.00 bill enclosed. Since it is illegal for me to have U.S. currency here in Viet Nam, I sent it to Veda so she can put it towards the set of pots and pans she just bought. Yup! She went out and purchased pots and pans — you might say she's kind of looking ahead and doing a little planning, huh! You know, I think I found myself quite a girl, if I do say so myself (I guess I could be considered slightly on the prejudicial side.)

   Got a letter from John, and he tells me he just got a brand new station wagon — he couldn't be planning on a large family, could he... I imagine he is pretty proud of his little daughter (¾ of the letter was about her), but that's only natural, huh? I'll probably be the same way when my turn comes, but that'll probably be quite a while from now —- then you'll be getting 'Old" — Grandma and Grandpa Pueschel! That even sounds old!!! Hope you don't mind me kidding you like that.

You know, I think I'm gonna give up birthdays — 23 sounds like a nice age to say for awhile, right in the middle, and I'll be a couple up on Dad and Jack Benny — after all, they're all of 39!!!

Got to run - take care, may God bless, and stay happy ———

" THE LOSER BUG"

May 1968 started out with some nice birthday thoughts of birthday cards, pots and pans, brand new station wagons, large families, and Grandpas and Grandmas. For Tom, the nice thoughts weren't allowed to last long as things were about to get much much worse.

For the month of May, the soldiers of F Troop, 8th Cavalry would feel the heat of battle singe their brows almost every day. The enemy would fight and fight again, and again and again. They would be relentless. The bullet holes in the sides and the running boards of the helicopters would multiply and multiply. The loss of gun-ships and other aircraft would pile up. And so would the loss of life. It would be a tough month for these soldiers, a tough month where the horrors of war would raise its head many times and in many different forms. The battles with the enemy in May of 1968 would include the battles of Ngok Tavak and the "rat-fuck bugout" of Kham Duc, resulting in evacuation and defeat.

Day 219, 15 May 1968 – "A couple of ships shot down."

Two gunships were shot down. Rescue helicopters did their job. The fighting was intense. *"That's one good thing about being in a unit like this one — if you do get shot down, chances are you won't spend much more than five minutes on the ground before you're on a rescue chopper on its way out of there."* Tom's words would prove to be prophetic, given what would happen to him just a few months later. Five minutes on the ground can be a very long time.

15 May 1968

   Dear Mom & Dad ——-

   Greetings and salutations from the land of mud and rice paddies! Glad to hear that you had a nice birthday and all — mine was sort of here and gone before I had time to slow down and feel a year older. I really didn't miss it much, though, so I guess it really doesn't matter much.

   Speaking of me missing weddings, I guess it's just poor planning or something but I guess it would be kind of hard to miss my own — that will have to be postponed for a while though, 'cause it looks like Uncle Sam is gonna keep me over here in never, neverland for a couple of months more than I expected – I guess experienced pilots are getting hard to come by over here right now, and so I won't be homeward bound till sometime in early December (9th or 10th or so). I haven't gotten Veda's reaction to this yet, but I don't imagine she's gonna be any too happy about it — as a matter of fact, I'm not jumping for joy either! I'm just thankful it's only a two-month extension instead of six, and I should be home for Christmas, which makes it a little easier to take! Who knows, Veda and I just might have a Christmas wedding if she hasn't forgotten all about me by then!

Things have been sort of popping around here lately — we've had a whole bunch of ships shot full of holes and we are all a bunch of nerves, but things are bound to get better — they couldn't get too much worse. Luckily, we haven't had any serious casualties, even though we have had a couple of ships shot down in the past couple of days. That's one good thing about being in a unit like this one — if you do get shot down, chances are you won't spend much more than five minutes on the ground before you're on a rescue chopper on its way out of there. As far as I'm concerned, though, as much as they shoot at me, the people who do must be awful shots — it always seems to be someone else who runs up against the better marksmen. Let's hope it stays that way, huh?

Don't go worrying too much about me – I'll be all right. I've lasted this long — I'll make it the rest of the way as long as I don't get careless, and believe me, I've become a very careful guy.

There is something I would appreciate if you could send it to me, and that is a small electric fan. It averages about 110° around here, and it would be great to cool me off a little and keep the mosquitoes off while I sleep. It doesn't have to be very big at all, just something to stir up the air a little. Ok?

I've got to run —— take care and may God bless —————

Love,

Kim

Pax vobiscum!

(Peace be with you!)

Tom's tour in Vietnam was extended two months to December 1968. Though he didn't say it in the letters, the extension was something he wanted to do, and, in some ways, it was his choice to stay. For two reasons: 1) he wanted to learn and fly the new Cobra helicopters that were soon to arrive, he loved to fly, and 2) he knew that the new pilots coming in were very green. He thought he could help them get oriented to the war before they got into big-time trouble. More than was done for his unit when they first arrived in Pleiku.

Battle of Kham Duc and the rat-fuck bugout

On May 10th, PAVN General Chu Huy Man and the 2nd Division attacked the US/Allied Special Forces camp at Kham Duc, located in a small district in the north of Quảng Tín near the Laotian border. North Vietnam's plan was to attack the US and allied defenders of the Special Forces camp to attract US reinforcements, overwhelm them, kill them, and film the entire scene as a propaganda tool. The timing of the attack was planned in sync with the first Paris peace talks and the attack was a furious attempt to undermine the talks.

The battle began on the morning of 10 May when enemy (PAVN) forces attacked two of the three hilltop outposts surrounding the Kham Duc camp. The attack was a full onslaught, and the enemy eventually overran the Ngok Tavak outpost which was located approximately five miles south from Kham Duc. An Australian-led Mobile Strike Command (MIKE) force which included a contingent of indigenous soldiers which were part of the Civilian Irregular Defense Group (CIDG), was ordered to hold their position at the Ngok Tavak outpost but could not. The fight did not last long, and allied forces took heavy losses. Forced to evacuate, the Australian commander moved his troops to Kham Duc to reinforce the Special Forces camp there. Meanwhile, a reinforced infantry battalion with an attached artillery battery of the 23rd Infantry Division (Americal) was airlifted into Kham Duc to defend the airstrip in preparation for a possible evacuation from Kham Duc. F Troop, 8th Cavalry was in the middle of this fight. PAVN attacks of the airstrip were repelled by some 350 sorties of tactical aircraft, including *Blue Ghost* helicopters, and the PAVN were not able to penetrate the camp.

The fighting continued for three days. On the morning of the 4th day, General Westmoreland made the decision that the cost of holding Kham Duc would be too high and evacuation was necessary. Thus, began the chaos and confusion of the "rat-fuck bugout." What ensued was an all-out effort to extract all the people in Kham Duc, both military and civilian. F Troop evacuated several companies of infantry, a couple of hundred mercenaries and assorted Command/control elements. In all, over 1500 military and civilian personnel were evacuated.

However, the evacuation was more rat-fuck than bugout, as it did not go well and proved very costly. Chaos on the ground abounded. Some units on the ground were not informed of the decision to evacuate, leading to total confusion as the evacuation was underway. Approximately 150 people (CIDG soldiers and their dependents) died when a C130 transport plane was shot down on takeoff (left photo below). Numerous other US troops were either killed or went missing as the enemy closed in.Soldiers were captured (one soldier captured would be held in captivity until 1973). The US military lost twelve aircraft, two helicopters, and a Cessna Forward Air Control (FAC) plane. In addition, thirteen marines from Ngok Tavak went missing when they attempted to escape on foot and never made the five-mile trek to Kham Duc. It was a major big time shitshow and the largest allied retreat of the war.

The chaos continued even after the camp was fully evacuated. With no one left to evacuate, the USAF dropped a Forward Air Control team into the camp and a USAF pilot, Lieutenant Colonel Joe M. Jackson, had to go back in and get them out. For his efforts, Jackson was awarded the Medal of Honor. A photo of the action as it happened was taken by a reconnaissance plane and is shown below (Dept of Defense photo). It shows Lt. Col. Jackson's C123 on the runway (top of photo) and the three men on the runway.

The results of the battle were 42 American dead, about 220 CIDG soldiers dead or missing, compared to an estimated 345 to 2,000 enemy PAVN dead.

While General Creighton Abrams downplayed the losses, calling it a "minor disaster," others called it, "an embarrassing defeat', "an unequivocal debacle", and a "decisive North

Vietnamese and Viet Cong victory".

C130 Shot Down (left); Lt, Col. Joe Jackson rescues three men on runway (right)

Day 223, 19 May 1968 – "Really got clobbered and lost four ships…one man died."

Four more gunships were shot down. One *Blue Ghost* was killed and many wounded. For all the soldiers and pilots, "*nervous exhaustion*" is setting in, but all they can do is buck up and keep fighting.

19 May 1968

Dear Mom & Dad ——-

I received your letter and the church bulletin this evening. It was good to hear from you again.

Things have been pretty much on the hectic side around here lately, and I have been flying just about every day. I think my last day off was sometime last week, but right now I can't seem to remember that far back. It's not so much that the enemy is keeping us so busy (although he does his share in that respect), but that we just don't seem to have enough pilots to go around anymore. Quite a few are in the hospital with wounds or a virus that's been going around. So far, I've escaped both, but if this pace keeps up much longer, I'm afraid I'm going to come down with a severe case of nervous exhaustion, and so will everyone else, for that matter. We really got clobbered not too long ago and lost four ships — as far as the crews go, we were sort of lucky in that only one man died, even though most of the others won't be flying for a while. As for me, my luck's still holding pretty well, so don't go worrying — besides, that side of things seems to have quieted down somewhat right now.

Well, it's pretty much official now that ten of us "originals" in this unit won't be going home until early in December, and my name is near the top of the list. I doubt if this will change very much, if any, in the future, 'cause they are really in a bind for experienced pilots, and those of us who are not married will be first to stay the extra couple of months or so. Also, seeing as how they have decided to keep us here awhile longer, they are also talking about sending us to Cobra school for a check-out in the Huey - Cobra gunship, and from what I hear, it's got one heck of a wallop in its firepower. Maybe that'll make old "Charlie" think twice about shooting back, huh? Just don't go worrying about me, ok? Sure, I'm disappointed, but it serves no purpose to gripe about it and two months isn't such a very long time, so I just take it as it comes and push my dreams a little further into the future. I'm kind of worried how Veda is going to take it — I know she worries about me quite a lot, for it shows in her letters and heck, she's got enough problems, so it is without me adding to them. It really bugs me 'cause there's nothing I can do and I feel so blasted helpless.

Yes, I received Carol's card a little while ago — quite a card too! Tell her thank you for me, and when I have time, I'll try and write to thank her myself. Also, thank you very much for the birthday cake and all the other goodies – they sure were good!!! I appreciate it very much.

I've got to run. Take care and may God bless, and don't worry about me - I'll make out AOK.

Love,

Jim

"One man died." — Final Mission of US Army Helicopter UH-1C Tail Number 66-00737

On 16 May 1968, in a mission in Quang Tin province, Sgt. Louis L. Bradley was the gunner in the four-member crew of UH-1C helicopter gunship, Tail Number 66-00737. As the gunner, Bradley was on the right side of the helicopter with Crew Chief Daugherty on the left. He was in a body harness and attached to the bulkhead of the helicopter with nylon straps through a D-ring on the body harness. This allowed the gunner and the crew chief to come out of their seats and stand on the skids, lean out, and fire below and behind the aircraft. The aircraft came under hostile small arms (AK-47) fire, causing the helicopter to crash. As the helicopter went down, Bradley was thrown out of his seat but stayed attached via his strap. In a horrible turn of events the ship rolled to the right on Bradley's side and his strap kept him in a position where the top of the cabin pinned him to the ground at his waist, leaving his lower body inside the cabin while his head and shoulders were outside. His spine was severed and he was killed when the helicopter became engulfed in flame. Hueys were built of aluminum and magnesium and burned very hot and the flames grew very fast. The surviving crew members were under intense enemy fire but were able to jump on two LOHs that landed nearby and escape. Bradley, pinned in the burning helicopter, was the only one of the crew to die. One of the pilots never got over the horrendous action as they could find no way to pull Bradley out of the helicopter in time. It was truly hopeless, Nothing could be done and it was a very ugly day in the war. John Shephardson witnessed the crash from 50 feet above in his helicopter and it has remained one of his most indelible memories, the "worst thing I ever saw," of his time in Vietnam.

Honoring his service. Honoring his memory.

   Louis Lloyd Bradley Jr., b. Metairie, LA, 12/27/1948 d. 5/16/1968 (age 19 years 4 months 20 days)

Louis L. Bradley Jr. KIA 16 May 1968

Day 227, 23 May 1968 – "As far as peace talks go ...may as well call them fairy tales."

Not enough pilots and crews. Those that were available suffered from nervous and physical exhaustion. The Paris peace talks fail before they start.

23 May 1968

Dear Mom & Dad ——-

Sorry I haven't been writing too much lately, but I haven't had any time off to speak of either lately. As it stands right now, we've got one more helicopter that we do pilots to fly — per se: five flyable gun-ships, only enough personnel to make up four crews. We had better be getting some new people in pretty soon or there's gonna be a whole bunch of pilots down with a bad case of nervous and physical exhaustion.R&R, wounds, and a virus that has been making the rounds has really cut man power down. Well, at least it's not making things boring, although it is pretty tedious and starting to border on drudgery. Otherwise, things are hunky-dory in Toonerville right now — we get shot at and we shoot back, cuss a lot, and manage to cram in a couple hours' sleep now and then, and as far as peace talks go, well...phooey — you may as well call them fairy tales, the way things look right now!!!

So much for my gripe — how's things on the old home front? Have you gotten used to your new car yet, or is it still too small??? I kind of lean more towards smaller cars anyway, so I may be a little prejudiced, but I think you'll like it after a while. You may not have as much room on the inside, but it sure is a lot easier to handle and to park, right?

I've got to run — just wanted to let you know I'm ok and still kicking up a storm cloud or two here and there (mostly here). Take care and may God bless ———

"Why me?" said the Little Bug. I wonder what would happen if everyone said that?

The Paris Peace Accords began on 10 May 1968 with American and North Vietnamese representatives meeting face-to-face for the first time in peace negotiations. Formal negotiations began on 13 May but immediately came to a standstill. The two nations continued to hold talks, with little or no progress.

While all the diddling and fiddling in Paris continued, the soldiers fought. Tom: *"...we get shot at and we shoot back, cuss a lot, and manage to cram in a couple hours' sleep now and then..."*

Day 241, 6 June 1968 – "New guys are a lot better off."

76 years since D-Day, June 6 1944.

Six new pilots arrived, and the experienced pilots teamed up with them to help them get to know their way around.

6 June 1968

Dear Mom & Dad ——-

I received the fan you sent today — thank you very much, it's just what I needed. Now maybe it will be a little more comfortable here — lately it has averaged about 100° during the day, and between 85° - 90° at night, so you can see why I'm glad to have it. Thanks very muchly.

Things haven't been going too badly around here lately — every once in a while it gets kind of hectic, but we now have six new pilots in my platoon, so the workload isn't quite as bad as it has been in the past. We'll still have to team them up with an experienced pilot for a few more months or so until they kind of get to know their way around. In a sense, these new guys are a lot better off than we were when we first got here — with us, there were no 'experienced pilots', and we kind of had to fumble our way around and learn for ourselves in a sort of hit or miss fashion. As I look back on it, we were, and still are, very lucky that we didn't get clobbered by the opposition in a number of incidents.

I've got to run — don't worry about me — I'll be ok. Take care and may God bless ————-

love,
Den

Day 241, 6 June 1968 – "a funny sort of letter"

It was a "funny sort of letter"... satire in a letter that Tommy sent to his Uncle Walter and Aunt Esther, who then sent it on to Tom's Mom & Dad (Erna & Dick)...a version of this letter circulated and was used by many soldiers as they neared the end of their tours. It is often cited on websites.

Dear Erna & Dick - Here is copy of Tommy's letter I promised you.

-2-

I came across a funny sort of letter that someone dreamed up as a sort of satire on the way we live over here, and I thought you might get a few laughs reading it. It reads as follows:

REPUBLIC OF SOUTH VIETNAM

Dear Civilians, Friends, Draft Dodgers, etc...

In the very near future, the undersigned will once more be in your midst, dehydrated and demoralized, to take his place again as a human being with the well known forms of freedom and justice for all; to engage in Life, Liberty, and the somewhat delayed pursuit of Happiness. In making your joyous preparations to welcome him back into organized society, you might take certain steps to make allowances for the crude environment which has been his miserable lot for the past twelve months. In other words, he might be a little Asiatic from Vietnameseitis and Overseasitis, and should be handled with care. Don't be alarmed if he is infected with all forms of rare tropical diseases. A little time in the "Land of the Big PX" will soon cure this malady.

Therefore, show no alarm if he insists on carrying a weapon to the dinner table, looks around for his steel pot when offered a chair, or wakes you up in the middle of the night for guard duty. Keep cool when he pours gravy on his dessert at dinner, or mixes peaches with his Seagrams VO.. Pretend not to notice if he eats with his fingers instead of silverware, and prefers C-rations to steak. Take it with a smile when he insists on digging up the garden to fill sand bags for the bunker he is building. Be tolerant when he takes his blanket and sheet off the bed and lays them on the floor to sleep on.

Abstain from saying anything about powdered eggs, whole milk, fried rice, or dehydrated potatoes. Do not be alarmed if he should jump up from the dinner table and rush to the garbage can to wash his dish with a toilet brush. After all, this has been his standard. Also, if it should rain, pay no attention to him if he pulls off his clothes, grabs a bar of soap and a towel, and runs outside to take a shower.

When in his daily conversation he utters such things as "Xin loi" and "Choi oi" just be patient, and simply leave quickly and calmly if by some chance he utters, "Di Di," with an irritated look on his face, because it means no less than, "Get the H___ out of here." Do not let it shake you if he picks up the phone and yells "Typhoon forward, sir," or says "Roger, out" for goodbye, or simply shouts, "Working!"

Never ask why the Jones' son held a higher rank than he did, and by no means ever mention the word "extend." Pretend not to notice if at a restaurant he calls the waitress, "Numba one girl," and uses his hat for an ash tray. Also, when in a store, be tolerant if he tries to bargain for an item at half it's listed price, or dives under the counter at the sound of

169

-3-

a siren or a car backfiring.

Above all, keep in mind that beneath his tanned and rugged exterior, there lies a heart of gold (the only thing of value he has left.) Treat him with kindness, tolerance, and an occaisional fifth of good liquor, and you will be able to rehabilitate that which once was (and is now an empty shell of) the happy-go-lucky guy you once knew and loved.

Last, but by no means least, send no more mail to the APO. Fill the refrigerator with beer, get the civvies out of mothballs, fill the car with gas, and get the women and children off the streets....

BECAUSE THIS MAN IS COMING HOME!!' !!! !!! !!

His signature

Well, I've got to run. Take care, may God bless, and stay happy.

Love,

Me

Day 245, 10 June 1968 – "Don't worry about me – us Gun-Pilots are invincible!"

As the days wore on, this gun-pilot was starting to think that he might make it back from the debacle, known as the Vietnam War, and he told all, including himself, *"Don't worry about me – us Gun-Pilots are invincible!"*

This was the first letter where Tom declared himself as *"Invincible."* As his time became shorter and the battles wore on, he would proclaim himself *"Invincible"* again and again.

Monday, 10 June 1968

Dear Mom & Dad ——-

Greetings and hallucinations from your prodigal son in Vietnam! I received the fan in the mail a couple of days ago – thank you very much, it is just what I needed. Now perhaps this place will be a little more livable.

There's really not too much to write about — things have sort of quieted down around her lately, but I can still sort of sense some sort of trouble brewing for the not too far off future.

We got a bunch of new pilots a while ago and it feels kind of funny.Most of them seem more like a bunch of kids still wet behind the ears but that is perhaps because I feel a lot older than I really am right now. Vietnam has a way of making you age very quickly – too quickly. Even so, when I fly with one of these new guys, I feel almost like an instructor, and most of the other 'old timers' seem to feel about the same. I think a lot of this is due to the fact that most of them received almost no flight time at all in a UH-1C helicopter during flight school, and since a loaded gun-ship has flying characteristics all its own as compared to other models in the UH-1 series, I guess it's pretty much like learning to fly a whole new aircraft to them. This, on top of learning tactics and what it feels like to be shot at, puts them more or less in the role of student for a while, rather than that of co-pilot. Another factor, I think, is the fact that most of them have an average of about 250 hours of flying time to their credit, whereas we 'old timers' average around 900-950 total flying hours, approximately 600-650 of those hours being combat time. That right there makes all the difference in the world, but it also places an added responsibility on our shoulders because the new people look to us old people for advice and for our experience to get them and us out of tight situations in one piece. There's really not much difference in our physical ages – they average around 20 years old, but there is a very noticeable difference mentally, for we have grown quite a ways beyond our years in these past six months of daily war and tense nerves. They are luckier than we were in so much as we did not have anyone to show us the way, but had to make it for ourselves in a hit or miss, trial by error proposition.Right now they think we know all the answers, but six months from now, when they are 'old timers', they will know as I do know that there are still a lot of questions that still remain unanswered.At any rate, it's a hell of way to make a living.

By the way, Veda has moved. She's now working five nights a week and is planning on attending summer school. She and two of her friends have rented an apartment for the summer. (address not shown)

She's quite a busy gal nowadays, with school and work, so I wouldn't count on her writing too much. I guess what she is trying to do is to keep herself busy to make time pass more quickly, and at the same time sort of assert her own independence, which is very important to her as it was to me a while back. I don't guess I really have to assert my own independence now, though, do I? I've been quite independent for quite a while.

I've got to run. Take care and may God bless, Don't worry about me — us gun-pilots are invincible!

US GUN-PILOTS ARE INVINCIBLE !

LOVE,

Den

There was a *"bunch of kids"* fighting this war. The average age was around 20 years old.

Day 245, 10 June 1968 – "Happy Birthday!"

Monday, 10 June 1968

Dear Larry ——-

I know this isn't much of a birthday greeting, but it's the best I can do right now. Happy Birthday, anyway, and don't do anything I wouldn't do! (That sure leaves the field wide open to suggestions)

I imagine school is just about the same, not any better but not any worse either, but it's a heck of a lot better than being over here. (At least, you don't get shot at, and you have pretty girls to look at and such!)

At any rate, Happy Birthday, for what it's worth. Take care and stay happy.

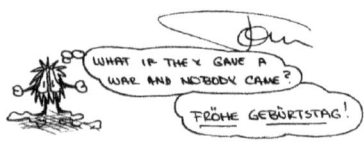

Tom wished his younger brother, Larry, a Happy Birthday. Larry turned 19 on June 14, 1968, and was finishing up his freshman year at the University of Massachusetts. He was holding on for dear life, literally, to his 2-S student deferment, as the looming Vietnam war hung over every able-bodied 18- and 19-year olds' shoulder in America. He heard more and more of the casualties of Vietnam, saw more of his high school classmates and friends off to war, and listened to many others in their objections to the war. It was fast becoming a war where nearly everyone knew someone "over there" or on their way. His friends were talking about burning their draft cards, applying for conscientious objector status, and some were contemplating just high tailing it to Canada. War protests were happening regularly, and Larry was being swept in, becoming more anti-war each day.

But with his older brother serving in Vietnam, and his parents on edge as the days passed, and thoughts of protest growing louder in his mind, his voice remained relatively quiet. Around him, the voices of protest rang in his ears. Sit-ins and marches happened every week, students chanting slogans, and yelling and screaming at the government and the military and at the military-industrial complex. The voices became a roar, and the unrest quickened its pace. For Larry, he would stay on the fringes of the protest world as best he could until Kent State and the student strike in 1970, which brought the war in Vietnam and the internal war at home into full focus.

Tom's thoughts on the matter, "What if they gave a war and nobody came."

Day 249, June 1968 — "The Frog"

Day 250, 15 June 1968 – "They were all getting cut to pieces, so we did all we could."

Tom wrote about receiving the Distinguished Flying Cross (DFC), which he received for actions performed on 9 February 1968. He was unimpressed and voiced this sentiment at the time: "To me, it's just something else I've got to pin on my uniform, and with a D.F.C. and a dime you can get a cup of coffee almost anywhere!"

Saturday, 15 June 1968

Dear Mom & Dad ——-

I'm glad you liked the little 'souvenirs' I picked up over here. Just don't go making too much of it, ok? I'm no hero, and I don't intend to become one.Besides, I got that stupid medal for being in the right place at the right time. We don't go up against fortified positions like that every day — as a matter of fact, when there's a 'fifty' down there, we usually try to call some jet fights in on it 'cause it's kind of a one-sided battle when you go up against a 50 caliber machine gun with a helicopter, and the odds are all on the other guy's side. The day I got the D.F.C. was a little different story, however, 'cause there were 3 companies of American G.I.'s down there and they were getting cut to pieces, so we did all we could, that's all. To me, it's just something else I've got to pin on my uniform, and with a D.F.C. and a dime you can get a cup of coffee almost anywhere! By the way, I've got about five more Oak Leaf Clusters for the Air Medal since then, so you can see how much time I put in behind the controls – most of the guys who came over here with me have about the same. I've got about 950-1000 hours of flight time now (total including flight school — only about 700 hours of combat time)

As far as being extended for two months – in a way I really don't mind too much 'cause if what I have learned over here can help some of these new pilots' chances of survival any, it will be worth it. They'll be on their own when I and my compadres depart from this never-never land, and they'll need all the help they can get. I'm not planning on doing much flying if I can help it!

The fan is working out nicely — it's just what I needed. As for anything else I need, <u>besides</u> Veda and food, well, I can't think of anything off-hand except perhaps some ideas of where I can take my future 'Chief of Staff' for a honeymoon — I've been thinking of Hawaii, but I'm afraid that might cost more than we will be able to afford – got any ideas?

I received a very nice letter from Gertrude Knopf and two of her Sunday School children yesterday. She says that she is trying to get them to show their love for Christ by writing to some of our people over here in Viet Nam, and I kind of think it's a nice idea.I have written back to her and to the two children who wrote to me, Robbin Ann Bollenbach and Kurt Kallmeyer. I imagine the kids especially the boy, will get a thrill out of getting a letter from a real live soldier and helicopter pilot, and besides, I kind of enjoyed writing anyway.

I've got to run — say Hi to everyone for me, and don't worry about me.

Take care and may God bless.

Day 259, 24 June 1968 – "Huey Cobra...going to have a ball flying it."

Tom was sent to the Bien Hoa Air Base, where he would receive training in the new Army helicopter, the Cobra. Tom loved flying and he was drawn to the new Cobra helicopters. The AH-1Gs were Attack Helicopters (AH) and that was their primary purpose. Sleeker, narrower, and faster than their counterpart UH-1C gunships, which were Utility Helicopters (UH) with many capabilities.

24 June 1968

Dear Mom & Dad ——-

Would you believe that I am now in Bien Hoa at the Cobra transition school, and already have the first day and an hour and forty-five minutes' flight in the 'Huey Cobra' behind me? For some odd reason, my CO decided to send me and a couple of the other guys down here to learn how to fly this totally new aircraft — could it be he finally took the hints I have been dropping every chance I got? Anyway, after that first flight this morning, I fell in love with it, and I sure am glad I'm here at the school — of course, it's really not too hard for me to fall in love with an airplane 'cause I fell in love with flying a long time ago, and it never got old to me, even after all this time. It's a great helicopter, and I'm going to have a ball flying it!

I'll be down here until about the middle of next month, so I imagine I'll have quite a stack of mail to answer when I get back to Chu Lai — here's hoping I'll have time to do so.

I seem to remember you asking in your last letter if I had lost any weight — about 30 pounds, as near as I can figure it, but I imagine I'll be gaining it back eventually once I return home again, if you and Veda have anything to say about it, huh?!?

I've got to go — got an early flight tomorrow, and I still have some book-learnin' to do. I'll write again soon — — —

Take care and may God bless —- don't worry about me, I'll be ok — —-

Love,
   TOM

The Cobra's cockpit measured just 36 inches wide. Compared with a Cobra, the slow but steady Huey Gunships could not match the added speed, maneuverability, and firepower.

AH-1G Cobra (left); UH-1C Huey (right)

Fact: Bell Helicopter built 1,116 AH-1Gs for the U.S. Army between 1967 and 1973, and the Cobras chalked up over a million operational hours in Vietnam; the number of cobras in service peaked at 1,081. Out of nearly 1,110 AH-1s delivered from 1967 to 1973 approximately 300 were lost to combat and accidents during the war. (Source: Wikipedia)

Day 274, 8 July 1968 – "Just a hunk of metal and a piece of ribbon, and not much more."

U.S. Congressman, the honorable Representative Silvio O. Conte (R-MA) sent Tom's family a letter of commendation for his efforts in Vietnam.

8 July 1968

  Dear Mom & Dad ——-

  Greetings and salutations from your prodigal son in Vietnam — I just got back from Cobra school a couple of days ago, and all now back at work again. That Cobra is quite a helicopter — it's almost like flying a fighter plane, and I get quite a kick out of flying it. It's funny but flying never seems to get 'old' to me — it still has the same appeal now as it did when I first started, perhaps even more so, since I am now a fairly accomplished pilot and I can sit back and enjoy it, and not have to sweat it through, so to speak, like I did when I was first learning. I am still learning, though, for in this business you never stop, and a day does not go by without learning something new. I wish I could explain the feeling I get when I fly, but I cannot, for it is something you have to experience for yourself, and not everyone will experience it. That's really nothing new, though, is it — I always did have my head in the clouds, didn't I?

It was very nice of Mr. Conte to write such a nice letter, but with all the big to do everyone seems to be making of it, I'm beginning to think that maybe I should have just kept my mouth shut and packed that medal away somewhere. I'm no hero, and I don't want to be — all I want is to get back home in one piece and try to find myself a place in this world where I can find happiness and contentment AND PEACE for myself and my future family, if I am to be so blessed.To me, a medal is just a hunk of metal and a piece of ribbon, and not much more — it doesn't show the blood, the sweat and the tears that so many have suffered over here, American and Vietnamese alike. They can keep all their medals and all their words of praise and find some way to bring a lasting peace throughout the world — that's the 'medal' I want, the only one.

I've got to run — take care and don't worry about me — I'll be A-OK.

MAY GOD BLESS YOU ALWAYS —
LOVE,
Jim.

Tom had seen first hand, the pain and suffering of war for both *"American and Vietnamese alike."* He would gladly have swapped all the medals in the world for *"a lasting peace throughout the world – that's the medal I want, the only one."*

Day 286, 21 July 1968 – "An old beat-up jalopy."

You might be fighting a war, serving your country in a foreign land, and risking your life every day, but you still had to keep up with those loan payments back home.

21 July 1968

Dear Mom & Dad ——-

Don't worry about that loan payment bill — I have already sent the forms you sent me in, so they should be getting them shortly, ok?

Well, we still haven't gotten our Cobras up here at Chu Lai, yet, but they are supposed to be sending us two on the 7th of August and the rest around the 20th. Till then, I'm back to pushing my old ship around, and even though it's like getting into an old beat-up jalopy, but at the same time, it's also like coming back to an old tried and trusted friend who hasn't once let me down. That old bird and I have spent a lot of time together, and I guess you could say we know each other very well. I'm gonna hate to say good-bye when these Cobras finally do get here.

I got a letter from Lil Wilhelm the other day and she says Dept-12 at N.B.B. has been invaded by the Pueschel clan — what happened – he hasn't got you working there too?!? (Only kidding).

There hasn't been too much going on here as far as the war is concerned lately, but even though it's kind of quiet, we still fly quite a few missions every day since we are primarily a recon unit. Something will probably break again soon, and then we'll be extra busy for a while until things quiet down again. Sure will be glad to get back to life in the 'world' again.

I've got to run — take care and may God bless ———- don't worry about me!

Love,

Dan

P.S. You've still got quite a way to go to catch up to this place — it's been averaging 120° – 125° lately!!!

Day 288, 23 July 1968 – "The shorter I have left to go, the 'chickener' I get."

"Take care and don't worry about me"

23 July 1968

Dear Mom & Dad ——-

Greetings and salutations from guess who! Things have been getting a little on the noisy side around here for the past couple of days, but it's not too bad. We were ready for them this time and they really got clobbered when they came down out of the hills again. From the looks of things, this little skirmish may not last too long, and it will probably go back to being quiet again soon. That's alright with me, though — the shorter I have left to go, the 'chickener' I get.

Got to run — take care and don't worry about me.

Love,
Jim

Day 293, 28 July 1968 – "From what I've heard on the news lately…"

Upon hearing the news from the home front, US Army soldier Thomas R Pueschel, stationed in one of the deadliest places on the planet, commented in one of his letters: "From what I've heard on the news lately, maybe I ought to start worrying about you people back home more – it sounds like it's more dangerous there than it is here right now – at least here you know they are out to get you and can shoot back when the occasion arises, but what do you do when you've got a sniper in your own backyard?"

Martin Luther King Jr. was assassinated on April 4, 1968. Robert F. Kennedy was assassinated on June 6, 1968.

28 July 1968

Dear Mom & Dad ——-

I haven't got too much time to write, but I wanted to at least drop a few line to let you know I'm ok and to thank you for the package —- it arrived yesterday intact! Thank you very muchly!!

From what I've heard on the news lately, maybe I ought to start worrying about you people back home more – it sounds like it's more dangerous there than it is here right now – at least here you know they are out to get you and can shoot back when the occasion arises, but what do you do when you've got a sniper in your own backyard? It kind of makes me stop and wonder if we might be better off if this whole world just shook itself apart. Also, seeing as how I'm planning on getting married sometime in the not too distant future, it makes me wonder if it would be fair to the children I am looking forward to raising, to bring them up in a world such as this one seems to have become. Have we begun to revert back to that primitive concept of life where only one law remains fast —- Kill or Be Killed, and to the winner go the spoils? God, I hope not, or I'll lay my weapon down and walk myself into a bullet right now.

Things have been relatively on the quiet side around here for the past week or so — once in a while we get a small skirmish here and there, or a tough mission into 'Indian Country' when the General decides he wants to know what's going on there near Laos or something. Why he always picks us for the job, I don't know, but I wish he quit it — I get cold chills when I think about flying over some of that territory!It's my job, though, I guess, and I'll do it, even if I don't like it!

Got to run —- Take care and may God bless. Don't worry!!!

Don't worry !!!.
Love,
Tom

Tom had good reason for getting "cold chills" when flying over Laos in June 1968.Since Laos was supposedly a neutral country, US troops were not stationed there and a no-fly zone was in place. If a pilot was shot down or somehow forced to land there were no support troops in the immediate area. Getting out and back to friendlier confines could be a long task.

When Tom came home, he would tell us to not believe what we heard in the news about not going into Laos and Cambodia. He told us that they made that run all the time.

Martin Luther King Jr. 1929-1968 (left); Robert F. Kennedy 1925-1968 (right)

Day 298, 2 August 1968 – "A set of nylon guitar strings."

Worn out guitar strings and a gift for Godson Kevin.

2 August 1968

Dear Mom & Dad ——-

I received your postcard today — looks like a nice place to visit — hope you all had fun. Things have been sort of on the hectic side around here — I haven't had a day off for about twelve days or so, and some occasions have been on duty for thirty-six hours straight. That stuff's gonna have to cease 'cause most of us are starting to get the shakes and that's not so good when you need a light control touch.

Looking at the calendar, it seems Kevin's birthday has snuck up on me before I knew it. Could you kind of pick something out for him for me. I'm not exactly in a position to do so at the moment and I'd sure appreciate it?

Oh, yes — one of these days if you get a chance, could you pick up a set of <u>nylon</u> guitar strings for me? The ones on the guitar I picked up in Japan are getting kind of worn out. I haven't had too much time to play it lately, but I manage to murder a couple of songs every now and then.

I've got to run – take care and may God bless – don't worry about me — I'll be ok.

Love,
Jen

Day 303, 7 August 1968 – "Don't worry too much about the bullet holes...section of flooring where the bullet came up between my feet."

7 August 1968

Dear Mom & Dad ——-

Greetings and salutations from your prodigal son in Vietnam. I'm glad you liked the slide I sent you – don't worry too much about the bullet holes – I haven't had too many put into my ship in quite a long time. That plate that I am holding in the picture is a section of the flooring where the bullet came up between my feet — I aged about ten years that day.In the near future, I will probably be sending along a whole bunch of 35 mm undeveloped film as soon as I get a chance to put it all together in a package and mail it. Most of them I took with a camera I picked up while in Japan — the camera, a Petri FT, cost me about a third what it would have cost me in the U.S.I believe the stateside price is fairly close to $200.00, so there are a few good things that come from being over here, I guess, though I would have much rather done without the camera, and not come in the first place.

Before I forget, I read something in the "Stars and Stripes" about Massachusetts having a $300.00 bonus for citizens of Massachusetts *who have served with the Armed Forces in Vietnam. I was wondering if you could look into that for me — an extra $300.00 will probably come in very handy, especially if I get married in the not too distant future. From what I hear, marriage can be a darn expensive proposition when you're first starting out.*

Things have been relatively quiet lately, but there is a sort of aura of danger in the air. You can almost feel the four horsemen of the Apocalypse sort of chafing at the bit to once again begin their ride across the sky. It's a nasty feeling, and something is going to break wide open before too long, if I don't miss my guess. I don't know, though – maybe I've just been over here too long and am getting jumpy in my old age.

I've got to run — don't worry too much about me — I'll be ok. Take car and may God bless ————-

LOVE,

Tom

Later, when Tom returned from Vietnam, when he was in the mood to talk about Vietnam, he would often tell us of the time bullets came up just beneath him, through the floorboards and into his seat, and how close they were to hitting him. But in the end, they were just holes, just like the many other bullet holes the helicopter took on. And the missions went on, holes and all.

Massachusetts did establish a bonus for those citizens who served in Vietnam. Chapter (Ch.) 646 of the Acts of 1968 stated that Vietnam veterans who served on duty in Vietnam were eligible for a $300 bonus. Tom did receive this bonus.

Day 311, 15 August 1968 – "I want to ride in that thing."

From stereo equipment to Cobras, and the *Blue Ghosts* getting the tough assignments. Tom again proclaimed, *"Don't worry about me...I'm invincible!!"*

15 August 1968

Dear Mom & Dad ——-

In a month and a half or so, you should be getting some packages in the mai from Agana, Guam. It will be the stereo tape deck and speakers etc. which I put an order in the mail for today. I imagine when it arrives, Kenny will be aching to get his hands on it, and it'll be ok with me as long as he doesn't go tinkering with it and splicing wires and such. That equipment cost me a pretty penny, even though it was only about half of what it would have cost in the states.It's professional equipment and very sensitive. It won't work, however, until the amplifier unit also arrives, and that will probably be the mail next month sometime, but will probably arrive there after the other stuff does. Then, all I'll have to get is a turn-table and I will have a complete stereo system to include ——- 1. stereo tape recording, 2. stereo Am–FM radio, 3. stereo record player; all of which can be built into a bookcase or something at a later date. At U.S. prices, it will be quite an expensive hunk of equipment, but it will have cost me only half that amount. This is something for which I have been saving for all the time since I arrived in Vietnam."

Today we will be picking up our second Cobra, and in the next couple weeks, the rest of them should come in. In a way, these Cobras will bring a lot of prestige to my unit, even though we, even now, enjoy a reputation of being one of the best, if not the best unit in the American Division, 'cause we will be the only unit in the Division, in the southern I Corps area, for that matter, to have Cobras. The one thing that bothers me, however, is that the General has a nasty habit calling on "Blue Ghost" whenever he has an exceptionally tough mission, and when we have our Cobras, I'm afraid he may well be more inclined to do so in the future. If we don't watch our step, we may well become opcon* to the General's discretion, instead of to the 1st Cav. (*opcon — under operational control). Right now, though, I imagine we've got the Division Artillery unit very mad at us. Yesterday, they were going to put on a firepower display (which they had been planning for four days prior), and, on the spur of the moment, they decided to include our Cobra (the only one we've got right now) at the beginning of their demonstration. Well, when the General saw what the Cobra could do, he said, "I want a ride in that thing!" and off he went, and with him went the Division Artillery's plans for a fire power demonstration. Oh, well, maybe next time, fellas??

I've got to run — take care and don't worry about me – I'm invincible!!!

and don't worry about me — I'm invincible!!!

Love,

Jim

When the General saw what the Cobra could do, he said, "I want a ride in that thing!"

Cobra – Attack Helicopter (AH)

Day 315, 19 August 1968 – "Last Light"

"Last Light" by TRP (Thomas R. Pueschel) 19 August 1968

Day 317, 21 August 1968 – "I get tomorrow off and, boy, am I gonna sleep!"

Tom now proclaimed, *"Don't worry about me — I'm invincible as well as indestructible!"* Veda was not writing as often and he was worried...

21 August 1968

Dear Mom & Dad ——-

Greetings and salutations from your friendly Duty Officer, me! Yup, tonight it's my turn to pull all night duty and make sure no bad guys make it past the perimeter fence while everyone else is asleep. All I can say is that's a good thing I only pull this once a month or so, 'cause I'm sure not made to stay awake all night, especially after flying all day. One good thing though — I get tomorrow off and boy, am I gonna sleep!!!

Things have quieted down some around here lately, but from what the intelligence reports say, all hell is gonna break loose pretty soon, if not here in Chu Lai, then someplace close by, and "Blue Ghost" will probably be right in the middle of it. We seem to have a knack for that sort of thing. That's ok, though — the less time I have left, the chickener I get, and the higher I tend to fly. It's kind of hard for them to hit you if you've got a layer of clouds in between...

I guess this summer went sort of fast for you people – summer always does sort of slip on by before you know it. It even went by sort of quick for me, but that's the way it is when you are always sort of busy — time doesn't have a chance to get on your hands and weigh you down, The last couple of months I have left over here though will probably seem like the longest of my entire life, but that too seems to be the rule when you are waiting so hard for a certain time to roll around.

I haven't gotten a letter from Veda in awhile, but I imagine she's pretty busy herself what with working, finishing up summer school, and getting ready for a new school year. Even so, I sure hope she hasn't forgotten about me — it's been such a long, long, long time since I left last October — a terribly long time, especially for a girl to sit and wait and worry.

I've got to go. Take care and may God bless — don't worry about me — I'm invincible as well as indestructible!!!

Day 320, 24 August 1968 – "brave, fearless, stone-hardened"

The Republic of Vietnam Gallantry Cross, also known as the **Vietnamese Gallantry Cross** or **Vietnam Cross of Gallantry**, was a military decoration of South Vietnam. The medal was created on August 15, 1950 and was awarded to military personnel, civilians, and Armed Forces units and organizations in recognition of deeds of valor or heroic conduct while in combat with the enemy.

For actions on 24 August 1968, CW2 Thomas R. Pueschel was awarded the Vietnamese Gallantry Cross. This was his second award of this medal.

Tom Pueschel receiving his 2nd Vietnamese Cross of Gallantry, in Tam Ky City

Republic of Vietnam Cross of Gallantry

Translated generally from Vietnamese to English, the citation reads as follows:

Non-Commissioned Allied Officer (T.R. Pueschel) is brave, fearless, stone-hardened, rich in combat experience. Especially in Operation QT/85-T Sub-Area Quang-Tin 24-8-1968 in Vung Ky-An, located at Quan Tam-Ky, Tinh Quang-tin. Although facing the enemy's powerful firepower, the non-commissioned officer fought in all dangers, each and every one of the dangerous positions. Side by side with Vietnamese soldiers with heroic courage, they fought fiercely, and made worthy contributions as follows:

-Killed 465 North Vietnamese soldiers on the spot

-Captured 3 soldiers/ North Vietnamese Communists.

-Collected 10 guns, 31 personal-weapon, ammunition and important military-equipment

Also awarded medals for that day were:

Frank Chepler

Ronald W. Nelson

Tucker C. Grant

Dennis H. Streeval

Jerry R. Griffin

David M. Blatts

Rober B. Pewih

George L. Jackson

Norman F. Jack

Fred G. Kinard

Morales F. Torres

Lawrence R. Larson

Bryan E. King

Day 321, 25 August 1968 – "Madder than a hornet and twice as mean."

The PAVN/VC launched the "Phase III Offensive" also known as the "August Offensive". The strategy was similar to the Tet Offensive in January and February, and to the May Offensive, with the aim of diverting U.S. forces from urban areas through attacking multiple border towns simultaneously, opening up the cities for attack. As with the other offensives, this proved to be a tactical failure for the North Vietnamese forces, as US forces stopped assault after assault.

Given the battlefield success, it was the soldiers' lament that it was time to stop "pussy-footing around and go get 'em." The frustration and anger were evident in Tom's letter home.

25 August 1968

Dear Mom & Dad ——-

This will be just a short note as I haven't much time to write. Things are pretty hectic around here right now, as you probably know from the news. We've got dinks coming out of the wood-work, and they sure don't seem too worried about running out ammunition. As far as I'm concerned, this little action right now sort of blows everyone's theories about making peace and halting the bombing all to hell, and if this is what it gets us, then we had better stop pussy-footing around and go get 'em before they get us. I just wanted to let you know that I'm ok and I'm madder than a hornet and twice as mean. I'm getting tired of getting shot at and right now, as far as I'm concerned, anyone outside that perimeter with slanted-eyes is a potential enemy, and if he moves wrong just once, he's dead! The way things are right now, that's the only way to play the game and come out of it in one piece —- shoot first, and ask questions later!

I've got to run —- take care and don't worry about me — I'm still indestructible!

—I'm still indestructible!
Love,
Ou

Tom proclaimed once again, *"I'm still indestructible!"*

Day 332, 5 September 1968 – "Not all that bad over here - could be walking instead of flying."

It was raining very hard and not good flying weather. *PS. "Only 93 days and a wakeup to go."*

5 September 1968

Dear Mom & Dad ——

Greetings and salutations from the other side of the world once again. We have been in the middle of a big operation for the past week or so and have been pretty busy lately, but things seem to be slowing down once again. Also, it looks like the monsoon season is beginning, for it has been raining almost continuously for the past three days, which doesn't make for very good flying weather. As a matter of fact, I should be flying right now but it is raining so hard at present that not even ducks dare venture out into it!

By the way, Dave Bressem's address should be 66 Silas Street if he hasn't moved since way back when. Actually, that's his mom's address, so you may not catch him at home as I seem to remember something about him going down to Walter Reed for some more work, but I'm sure you can get a hold of him through his Mom at any rate.Let me know if you do,ok?

Yes I remember the Kloibers very well, and the young fella who is so interested in helicopters wouldn't be that little guy who was always getting into mischief like "Dennis the Menace" way back when, would it? Well, if he really is so interested, maybe when I come home I can tell him all he wants to know. I should have a bunch of manuals and stuff on the subject somewhere amongst all the junk I've accumulated since I started flying. I wouldn't be too surprised if someday he ends up flying too. Remember how I was always interested in airplanes ever since I was knee-high to a grasshopper. Now, I guess it's in my blood to stay.

Well, looks like the rain is going to let up a little, so I guess I had better start getting ready to go fly. Take care and don't worry about me — it's not all that bad over here (I could be walking instead of flying).

Love,

Jim rou...

P.S. Only 93 days and a wake up to go!!

Day 336, 9 September 1968 – "One thing we don't have …is cookies."

Tom became sick, having contracted pneumonia, and was sick enough to be confined to a bed for a week.

9 September 1968

Dear Mom & Dad ——-

Sorry if I haven't written for a while, but I haven't been feeling very well lately. As a matter of fact, for the past week or so I've been sick in bed with pneumonia. I know it sounds crazy to have pneumonia in the middle of a tropical climate like this one, but that's what the "Doc" said it was, and I haven't been able to sit down hardly at all 'cause of all the penicillin shots he gave me. I'm ok, now, though so don't go worrying,ok? As a matter of fact, he put me back on flying status this morning.

I received your package yesterday – thank you muchly for all the goodies and such — I'll let you know how I like the stuffed peppers as soon as I try them, ok? By the way, old "Snoopy" is sitting here on my desk watching me write this letter.I think I'll take him for a ride when I go fly next time.

There's really not much I need in a package — living on a pretty simple scale, and most of the necessities, such as shaving cream, soap and stuff are pretty easy to come by. One thing we don't have, though, is cookies. Some of those would go pretty good, and they don't have to be home-made either — I know it's a lot of trouble to go and bake them. Otherwise, I really can't think of too much, ok?

I've got to run —- take care, and don't worry about me — I've made it this far —- I'll make it the rest of the way!

I miss you all. May God Bless ————————

Love,

P.S. Wish Mark (youngest brother) a Happy Birthday for me. I wish I could do more than just write it in a letter like this, but I cannot, so ——-HAPPY BIRTHDAY, MARK!!!

Tom's youngest brother, Mark Pueschel, would serve in the U.S. Air Force reserve, as a firefighter, from 1978 - 1984. He served 3 years active and 3 years inactive and was honorably discharged in 1984. Fortunately, the Vietnam war was long gone by then.

Day 342, 15 September 1968 – "Still here and wishing I wasn't."

The missions shifted south, much of it to Quang Ngai and Tam Ky. Tom proclaimed again, "I'm invincible!"

15 September 1968

Dear Mom & Dad ——-

Got your letter this evening when I returned from Quang Ngai, where we have been operating for the past few days. Glad to hear you were able to make it to the wedding.

***No** (Tom emphasized in bold in his letter), Veda isn't very much of a letter writer — as a matter of fact, I only average about one letter every week and a half or so myself, but in your case, well, for one thing I think she feels sort of funny writing to you from the mere fact that she really doesn't know you too well. Also, it is kind of hard to write to your boyfriend or girlfriend's parents.Another thing is that she has been quite a busy girl this summer what with working nine hours a day and also taking some courses in summer school, plus, from the sound of her letters, I think she's got a couple problems of her own that she hasn't told me about yet.*

As for me, well, I'm still here and wishing I wasn't, but that's life! Time goes by — I just have to wait it out, that's all.

I've really got to run – tomorrow promises to be a long day ——

just wanted to drop you a few lines to let you know I'm ok and still kickin' up a fuss.

Take care and don't worry 'bout me — I'm invincible!

I'm INVINCIBLE !

LOVE,

Jeu

Day 343, 16 September 1968 – "Just don't go worrying – I'll be ok."

Just don't go worrying — I'll be Ok.

16 September 1968

Dear Mom & Dad ——-

Enclosed is a check for $220 —- it's repayment of a loan I made to one of the guys a while ago, so how about putting it in my checking account or something, ok?

I really haven't too much time or much to write about — things are pretty much the same, with no real change. Just don't go worrying — I'll be ok.

Got to run —— take care and may God bless ——————-

Love,

[signature]

Day 349, 22 September 1968 – "I'll have to start brushing up on my German."

22 September 1968

Dear Mom & Dad ——-

I received your letter yesterday with the news about Bob Gosselin receiving the Silver Star — see, I'm not the only one who sticks his neck out every once in a while!!

As far as me getting a teaching job, as you put it, I kind of doubt that very much. You see, yesterday I also received a TWIX (kind of a forewarning from the Department of the Army on my next duty assignment after I leave Vietnam. I'll be getting about thirty days leave back in the States, and then, on 18 January 1969, I'm due to report for duty in Germany, which will be a tour of approximately twelve (12) months. Looks like I'll have to start brushing up on my German, huh? Actually, this came as quite a surprise, 'cause it is highly unusual for someone to be sent to Europe from here without submitting a request for that assignment.As a matter of fact, I had submitted a request for Fort Knox not too long ago — wasn't too far off, was I?All in all, though, I'm kind of happy about it 'cause I've always wanted to see Germany, and while I'm there I'll probably be able to see the rest of Europe also. One thing worries me, however, and that is what Veda is going to think about it. If we get married while I'm home on leave, then she'll be able to go there with me —- if not, well, then I'm afraid things will be all washed up between us, 'cause it's been a long year already without another one to follow. This is something that will have to be worked out between us, though, when I return home — then we shall see, I guess. But, be ye hereby forewarned — you may have ro be prepared to attend your oldest son's wedding come this December!!

I don't know yet exactly where in Germany I'm supposed to be going, but I'll let you know as soon as I find out. From what I can figure out by educated guessing, it could be Heidleberg, Frankfurt, or Augsburg, but I cannot be entirely sure.At any rate, it ought to be quite an interesting assignment regardless of where it will be.

Also, out of the $220.⁰⁰ I sent in one of my previous letters, could you put about $100.⁰⁰ or so in my checking account – I'm going to be writing a check for that much pretty soon when I order a turn-table and its accessories for my stereo system which has already been ordered. Ok? Got to run ——— take care and may God bless

————-

Love,
Jen

Day 352, 25 September 1968 – "Just plain don't have time for much of anything except war."

25 September 1968

Dear Mom & Dad ——-

Just a few lines to say hello — I received your last couple of letters last nigh and I thought I'd write now while I have time — later I may not.Right now I am sitting in the Command Post at our forward fire base, waiting for the rain to let up a little so we can fly. It looks as though the monsoons have finally arrived, for it has been raining almost continuously for the past four days, but at least I don't have the sniffles anymore. We had a couple of days that were real warm a while ago, and it seems to have dried out my sinuses as well as the countryside, but now it is a veritable sea of mud again. This place is either one of two extremes — dusty or muddy – never somewhere in between.

I know a lot of my letters really have nothing much to say, but I try to write as often as I can 'cause I know you people back there are worried, but don't go worrying too much if a letter doesn't come every once in awhile — things have a way of getting pretty hectic at times, and we just plain don't have time for much of anything except war.

As far as that general goes who is always sending us out on special missions, well... he's the Commander of the Americal Division. and I imagine it is pretty much because of my unit's combat record (we have been put in for two Presidential Unit Citations, one Valorous Unit Citation, and one unit commendation so far) and also, simply because of the fact that we are the only unit in the Americal Division who have Cobras so far.

It looks as though the rain is starting to let up, so I imagine I'll be going out on a mission pretty soon.

Take care and may God bless — don't worry about me – I'll be ok!

Love,
Jim

P.S. "Snorty" now has about 6 hours of flight time in the Huey-Cobra!

Day 353, 26 September 1968 –
"Couple tubes of mustache wax."

26 September 1968

  Dear Mom & Dad ——-

  No sweat on the money — if you need any more, I've got a whole bunch more in my bank account too!! I don't think there'll be any sweat on that $100.00 I wrote about earlier — I imagine I've probably got a little extra in the checking account that will cover that and the car payments also.

  Speaking of my car — if you can sell it, go ahead — I don't think it's going to do me all that much good in Germany. I'll probably end up buying a V.W. while I'm over there to get me around and then sell it when I leave in 1970.

  Before I forget, could you send along a couple tubes of mustache wax, if you get the chance. Right now I've got a handle-bar that goes every way but right!

  Got to run — take care and may God bless ——————

Love,

Dan

Day 363, 6 October 1968 – "Command and Control"

The Command-and-Control ship, new troop commander and twice as many radios. "Huey" versus "Cobra".

6 October 1968

Dear Mom & Dad ——-

First of all, let me answer your questions about the UH-1 helicopter before I forget. The UH-1A, UH-1B, UH-1C, UH-1D, & UH-1H are all "Huey" helicopters that are used in the Army. The Air Force and the Marines have Hueys also, in the "E" & "F" models being the primary troop & cargo & med-evac choppers, and the "B" & "C" models used as gunships. All the Hueys are of a basic construction and thereby interchange various parts — the differences between the (...ran out of ink) various models (A,B,C,D,H) are in the engines, rotor-heads, & tail down construction. The UH-1A was the first model to come out and is now obsolete. The UH-1H was developed to replace the UH-1D, the major change being a more powerful engine & larger rotor blades — the UH-1C was developed to replace the UH-1B, the major difference being in the rotor-head and tail chamber, increasing its payload and airspeed and maneuvering capabilities.The Cobra (AH-1G – AH = Armed Helicopter) is a different breed of cat from all the rest entirely, but still retaining many basic Huey characteristics and interchangeable parts.However, the Cobra is primarily a fighting helicopter with many characteristics similar to those of a WWII fighter plane. It has higher air speeds, can do maneuvers which a helicopter ought not to be able to do, and is a finely tuned and delicate piece of machinery, and a highly sophisticated aerial assault weapons platform. In some ways, it even looks like a fighter, being only 36 inches wide and having a long, sleek silhouette. To me, it is a joy to fly and I feel more like a fighter pilot than a helicopter pilot, but as if not too long ago, I am back to flying a UH-1C (we have only two now) with my new C.O. in the other seat. We use this as a Command and Control ship, and the reason they put me in it is the troop commander just took over not too long ago, and he wanted someone with a lot of gunship experience to help keep him "out of trouble." He's still sort of feeling his way around, and besides, if you put one of the newer guys in there, he'd probably go nuts in a short while — we carry twice as many radios than normal, and with all those going at the same time, it gets kind of hectic, even when you're used to it. I really don't mind — all I'm doing is waiting out my time and keeping my head down.

Hope I answered your questions well enough — got to run - may God bless, and don't worry!!!

love,

Jim

Day 366, 9 October 1968 – "futility and insanity"

It is not a life but mere existing...

9 October 1968

Dear Mom & Dad ——-

What two packages did you get? I really have no idea how many there will be — there should be quite a few from Guam containing a stereo tape deck, speakers and such, and also a couple packages from New York containing a turn-table — right now I have an FM-AM stereo tuner-amplifier with me which will be in the mail as soon as I get a chance — none of the other stuff will work without it 'cause it's through this that the power is supplied to the rest of the system.

From the tone of one of your last letters, I get the impression that because of this impending assignment in Germany I may rush into a few things such as getting married. Well, as far as that goes, it is still sort of up in the air with Veda and me at least until I return and we have a chance to be alone with each other and talk it through. We've been engaged for over a year, now, and it has been a long and lonely year for both of us — we both realize that many things may have changed since we were last together, and that is why we make no definite plans —- however, with only a month or so, things will have to be decided and done rather quickly — perhaps more quickly than we'd like, but done regardless out of necessity. Therefore, when I return home, we will have to decide definitely, and she will either come to Germany as my wife, or I will be going very much alone with a diamond engagement ring to dispose of for I cannot ask her to wait for another year — this past one has been too long and too lonely as it is, and I do not want to have to wait another year either, for I'm tired of living through letters and wishing I were somewhere else —- if she marries me, then my home, our home, will be wherever we happen to be, and this has been my dream for a long time — to be able to say: "This is my home!" However, if the decision is made in the negative, I am not saying that our relationship will end right there for all time, but rather, that we both will again be free (I don't know if free is the right word to use) to lead our own lives and perhaps when I return from Germany we could start anew — perhaps not, but at least in this way, we would both know pretty much where we stand, and can lead our own lives down whatever paths we choose to follow. If I have not learned anything else here in Vietnam, I have learned this —— to live each day as if it were your last, and do not plan too far in advance except only tentatively, being flexible and readily adaptable to changes as they occur. I did not request Germany, and I wanted to take things slowly — perhaps marrying four or five months after I returned, if we were still agreeable to it, but now, this cannot be, and it is a miserable existence – (it is not a life but mere existing) to have an ocean and thousands of miles between yourself and the person whom you love and are engaged to marry. I love Veda, Mom, and I can say that with truthful and definite conviction – as to how she feels ——well, she says she loves me, but as to her definite convictions I cannot say — only she can say that. She is a little on the scared and unsure side as far as

223

marriage is concerned, mainly. I think because of what happened between her parents and the mark it left on her. It wasn't a very pleasant experience for her, and she was at the right age where it affected her deeply. All in all, however, things will have to be decided when I return — I have never felt more hopeless than I do now with 11,000 miles and the Pacific Ocean between me and where my heart and mind abide. Even so, I think both Veda and I are mature enough to see the pitfalls and make our decisions for the best as we see it.Neither of us are prone to jumping without looking first, and we have pondered, and are pondering still, our relationship and the decisions we will soon have to face. I believe I have grown up quite a lot since I came over here, for you cannot help but mature quickly with the countless life and death decisions you have to make in a fraction of a second over here every time you go out on a combat mission, and most of my decisions must have been good ones, for I am still alive and in one piece — if I had let indecision creep in, I would have been dead long ago. I've made many mistakes, true, but I have learned to profit by these mistakes, and as you go along, the mistakes seem to become fewer and the decisions easier, but not without cost, for after a year over here, I feel like a tired, worn-out, very old man, caught up in the futility and insanity of meeting my fellow-man in anger and hate on the field of conflict. Somewhere along the line, I feel l lost my youth.

I've got to run —— take care and don't worry ————

— Love,
Jim

Day 373, 16 October 1968 – "Besides, I'm Invincible."

Getting ready to go home ...

16 October 1968

   Dear Mom & Dad ——-

   A couple of days ago I received my orders, so now I guess it is official as far as me going to Germany. At least, I'll be able to be home for Christmas this year, anyway.According to the orders I should be bidding Vietnam a final farewell and steppin aboard that great iron bird to freedom on or around the 4th December. That means I should be back in the U.S. and all processed out by the 6th. I think what I probably will do is stop by New Albany on the way so I can get together with Veda and see if we can work things out one way or another — we aren't going to have too much time as it is, and we've got a lot of talking and deciding to do. If you want, I could call you from San Francisco or wherever they happen to let me go on leave, or I could wait till I got a little closer, if you prefer. Somewhere in the middle of everything else, I'm going to have to squeeze in some Christmas shopping also, I just remembered —- I don't think there are going to be enough hours in the day when I get home, but I don't guess that'll be anything new after the way *things can get to popping around here. Right now I'm running around sort of like a chicken without a head trying to get some things done before-hand without enough time to do it all. It's amazing how much junk a guy can accumulate in a year and how much red tape there is to wade through just to get home — would you believe I also have to get <u>five</u> shots before leaving here? I'd rather take on a V.C. division than face "Doc" and his needle! I hope you don't mind if I go ahead and sell that fan you sent me to one of the new guys — they are hard to come by over here and I have had a bunch of offers already.A lot of the stuff I have accumulated I will probably either sell, give away, or throw out — I'm planning on traveling as light as possible — it makes it easier going through customs and besides I hate carrying a suitcase! A lot of stuff I will be mailing home, such as my tape recorder and some extra uniforms etc. ok?*

I've got to run — take care and don't worry about me – I got this far —- I'll make it the rest of the way!!! Besides — I'm invincible!

Love,
Me

Day 377, 20 October 1968 – "planning on traveling light when it comes time"

16 October 1968

Dear Mom & Dad ——-

Those packages you received from New York should be my turn-table.I would appreciate it if you would open them up and check the condition of the equipment — it could have been damaged during shipment. There should be the turn-table itself, the base for it, a dust-cover, and a stylus. Sometime soon, you should also be receiving some stuff from Guam – an Akai "360-D" tape deck, two "SW-130" speakers, two "DM-13" microphones, two "AMS-5L" mike stands, and a whole bunch of patch cords.I've still got my FM-AM tuner-amplifier here — I just haven't had a chance to mail it, as yet. Also, when I get the chance, I will be mailing a bunch of fatigues and stuff home — I'm planning on traveling light when it comes time to leave this place! Oh, Yes, also within the next month or so, there should also be another package in the mail from Hong Kong — I ordered some suits and sweaters through a cut-rate plan available to us over here – you get so many suits etc. for a set price, no matter what material you pick out — all tailored to fit you — I figure that in comparison to U.S. prices for the same stuff, I have saved about $150.00! Actually, for the price of two good suits or less expensive material than what I picked, I am getting two suits, one sport-coat,two sets of slacks, and two sweaters — can't beat that!

Right now we are sitting here waiting for a monsoon to pass over — we've got high winds and heavy rain — back home it would be a hurricane, but here it's a monsoon. Actually, it has been raining pretty steadily for the past seven days only letting up to an occasional light drizzle of short duration. When I was out flying yesterday, it looked as though half of Vietnam was under water, and the other half threatening to sink any minute! You've never seen it rain like it does here —— take the heaviest rain we've ever had back there, multiply it by 10, and you might come close —- it's like being under a high-pressure fire hose!

As far as the mustache goes — well,I don't think you'll have to worry too much about it — I grew it just for the heck of it and well, because it's something just about everyone does over here at least once — kind of like a fad. I'll probably wear it home just to get your reaction and then shave it off — it really doesn't suit me anyway — I feel too conspicuous with it , and that's something I don't really care to be. Over here, it's not too bad 'cause most everyone's got one, but back home I'd feel like some sort of hippie, and besides, it can be a pain in the neck at times. By the way, you might be interested to know I am now shaving with a straight-razor, but I still need a lot of practice — I still manage to cut myself at least twice, and I use safety razor to shave my neck for fear of cutting my own throat! Just something else I do for the heck of it.

Got to go. Take care and may God bless ————

LOVE,

Day 386, 29 October 1968 – Shot Down! In Quang Ngai!

During the past few months, Tom repeatedly proclaimed that he was *"invincible"* and *"indestructible,"* six times in all. Those claims nearly ran out on the day of 29 October 1968.

By this time, much of the action for the *Blue Ghosts* had shifted south. With just thirty-seven days to go in his tour in Vietnam, Tom's mission in Quang Ngai took a perilous turn.

Shot Down!

On this date, Tom was piloting an armed UH-1C helicopter providing close air support for ground operations near the village of Quang Ngai. While performing a screening mission for friendly ground forces, his aircraft took on intense enemy ground fire, causing the engine to falter.

Realizing the seriousness of the situation, he sent out a distress call to other aircraft in the area, informing them of the situation and his approximate location.As the helicopter plummeted to the ground, he assisted the aircraft commander in selecting a suitable landing area.

After landing, he disregarded the heavy enemy fire and remained in the aircraft to insure that all electrical and fuel switches were off, preventing further damage to the aircraft by fire. Moving out of the aircraft, he directed the crew in establishing a perimeter around the aircraft. Completing this task, he marked the hostile positions with smoke grenades and directed gunships in placing suppressive fire on the insurgents, effectively neutralizing the enemy fire.

When the relief helicopter arrived, he directed the crew in the evacuation of all ammunition, weapons, and classified material before boarding the aircraft itself.

In the face of this tremendous pressure, Tom distinguished himself on the battlefield, ultimately bringing the crew and himself to safety.

(Note: The description of this action was extracted from General Orders, Number 9279, dated 3 December 1968, <u>AWARD OF THE DISTINGUISHED FLYING CROSS,</u> *signed by* R.S. Temple, JR. 1LT, AGC<u>)</u>

Distinguished Flying Cross, 1st Oak Leaf Cluster

CW2 Pueschel distinguished himself by exceptionally valorous actions on 29 October 1968 while serving as a pilot with F Troop, 8th Cavalry. For heroism while participating in aerial flight as evidenced by voluntary actions above and beyond the call of duty in the Republic of Vietnam, CW2 Thomas R. Pueschel was awarded the Distinguished Flying Cross (DFC, 1st Oak Leaf Cluster). This was the second time he was awarded the DFC.

The DFC award further stated: "Chief Warrant Officer Pueschel's personal heroism, professional competence, and devotion to duty are in keeping with the highest traditions of the military service and reflect great credit upon himself, the American Division, and the United States Army."

Tom's DFC with Oakleaf Cluster

Day 389, 1 November 1968 – "I'm still invincible!"

Still Invincible! In this letter, there was no mention of the furious action that happened just two days before when his helicopter was shot down, or about his actions leading to the awarding of the Distinguished Flying Cross (DFC). Just another day in-country. And he was still "invincible!"

Instead, he was focused on the next thing — the new "Blue Ghost" propaganda pamphlet, shown below. These pamphlets were scattered in their area of operation.

1 November 1968

Dear Mom & Dad ——-

I received your letter with my tax refund yesterday —- thanks for sending it along. Don't worry — I'll call when I get back to the states — it may be from Fort Lewis, Washington (where I imagine I will be processed back into civilization again) or maybe from Seattle or San Francisco ——- whichever airport I happen to go to in order to get the rest of the way. I imagine I'll probably have to catch a flight from the West coast to Chicago, and from there to Standiford Field in Louisville, Kentucky, so I can see Veda and work things out with her —- from there it'll be a short hop, skip, & jump to Bradley Field, probably via New York. See, I've got things all planned out already! I've been looking forward to going home for a long time now, and it's hard to believe the time is almost here.

Enclosed you will find a copy of our new "Blue Ghost" propaganda pamphlet. We scatter these all over our areas of operation to sort of let everyone know we don't fool around. The "MA XANH" means "Blue Ghost" in Vietnamese, and the pamphlet says in essence that they should beware, for the "Blue Ghost" will get them if they coerce with V.C. It also tells that we will receive defectors with "open arms" and no harm will come to them. Guess who drew the "Blue Ghost", by the way!!!

I got a notice in the mail today from the Akai people that my tape equipment has been shipped finally, so it should be arriving there sometime soon — also I managed to mail my tuner-amp to you a while ago, and that should complete the system. I'd appreciate it if you would also check over the stuff when it arrives – the stuff from Akai people in Guam will come in four (4) packages — the tuner and in one (1) from here. I am enclosing the notice from Akai and also the insurance slip for the tuner-amp, OK?

I've got to run ——— take care, may God bless, and don't worry about me — I'm still invincible!!!

Love,

ĐỪNG ĐỂ CON " MA XANH " ẤM HẠI BẠN

CÁC BẠN VIỆT-CỘNG TRONG KHU VỰC NẦY CHÚ-Ý !!!

Hãy nhìn kỹ cái chết trước mắt. Đáng lý ra những bạn nầy đã có thể tránh khỏi cái chết, nhưng chính họ đã dại-dột dẫn bước theo một chủ-nghĩa phi-nhân nên họ phải rước lấy thảm-họa. Chính hỏa-lực Đồng-Minh đã tiêu-diệt họ. Nhưng trước khi tử thần đến, bạn có thể hồi-chánh với Chính-Phủ Việt-Nam Cộng-Hòa bằng cách trốn thoát khỏi đơn-vị. Chôn dấu vũ-khí một nơi để sau nầy tìm lại lãnh thưởng. Nếu không có vũ-khí vẫn có thể hồi-chánh. Ra hồi-chánh với các viên chức Việt-Nam Cộng-Hòa hay lực-lượng Đồng-Minh. Hãy trở về với Chính-nghĩa Quốc-Gia.

7 — 582 — 68

"Blue Ghost" propaganda pamphlet–Front (top) and Back (bottom)

234

Translation in essence is as follows.

Front: *Don't Let the Blue Ghosts Get You!*

Back: *VIETNAMESE IN THIS AREA – ATTENTION! Take a close look at the death before your eyes. Your friends could have avoided death, but they themselves were foolishly committed to inhumanism, that they had to take the disaster. It was the Allied forces that destroyed them. But before death comes, you can return to the Government of the Republic of Vietnam! Escape from the unit. Bury your weapons in one place to find the reward later. If you don't have a weapon, you can still recover. Return to the government of the Republic of Vietnam or the Allied forces. Return to the National Cause.*

Day 390, 2 November 1968 – "Tax refund."

2 November 1968

Dear Mom & Dad ——-

I'm sending that tax refund back signed —- go ahead and put it into my checking account or something. Ok?

Bye,

Day 398, 10 November 1968 –Bronze star award-"a signal of sacrifice, bravery, and honor while serving their country"

Warrant Officer W1 Thomas R. Pueschel, United States Army, was awarded the prestigious Bronze Star for *"meritorious achievement in ground operations against hostile forces in the Republic of Vietnam during the period October 1967 – November 1968."*

The Bronze Star Medal (BSM) dates back to World War II. It is one of the higher ranking awards a service member can receive for heroic and meritorious achievement performed in an armed conflict.

C I T A T I O N

BY DIRECTION OF THE PRESIDENT
THE BRONZE STAR MEDAL

IS PRESENTED TO

WARRANT OFFICER W1 THOMAS R. PUESCHEL, W3155673
UNITED STATES ARMY

who distinguished himself by outstandingly meritorious service in connection with military operations against a hostile force in the Republic of Vietnam. During the period

OCTOBER 1967 TO NOVEMBER 1968

he consistently manifested exemplary professionalism and
initiative in obtaining outstanding results. His rapid assessment and solution of numerous problems greatly enhanced
the allied effectiveness against a determined and aggressive
enemy. Despite many adversities, he invariably performed
his duties in a resolute and efficient manner. Energetically
applying his sound judgement and extensive knowledge, he has
contributed materially to the successful accomplishment of
the United States mission in the Republic of Vietnam. His
loyalty, diligence and devotion to duty were in keeping with
the highest traditions of the military service and reflect
great credit upon himself and the United States Army.

Day 399, 11 November 1968 – "I voted for the one whom I thought would do the least harm."

"…there wasn't a very good selection of candidates, so I voted for the one whom I thought would do the least harm."

11 November 1968

Dear Mom & Dad ——-

Sorry I haven't written in so long — things have been sort of on the busy side around here, and besides, I've been slowly packing and sorting etc. in anticipation of going home — couldn't be that I'm looking forward to leaving this place, could it?

Well, the election is finally over, and I see the man I voted for got it. In my opinion, however, there wasn't a very good selection of candidates, so I voted for the one whom I thought would do the least harm. I'm sure glad I'm not in his shoes, though —- he's got one hell of a tough job facing him.

Yesterday, my door-gunner came down to my hooch to talk a few things over with me, and something he said sort of has me worried —- when he saw the picture of Veda and me on my desk, he couldn't believe it was me — he said I look a great deal younger

239

and different in the picture than I do now, so now he's got me looking in the mirror every once in awhile looking for lines and stuff — personally, I think he's all wet — that picture's only about a year old and I hope I haven't changed all that much in so little time! I suppose the mustache adds a couple of years or so I hope.

I'm not putting too much faith in this new bombing halt — I've got a funny feeling that the V.C. will only build back up again and come again harder —- unless, of course, we hurt them too badly during their last offensive — then think they will probably go back to guerrilla warfare and terror tactics which is the dirtiest and ugliest sort of warfare known to man. As for this conflict ever being over, I think not —- not for a long, long time and about the only reprieve we can hope for in another truce as in Korea, and you know as well as I that isn't much of a truce.

Got to run —— take care and may God bless ———see you soon!!!

President Lyndon Johnson announced that the bombing operation in North Vietnam, known as Operation Rolling Thunder, would halt on November 1st in anticipation of renewed peace talks in Paris between South and North Vietnam. Johnson was willing to halt the U.S. bombing of the North, and with the Soviets applying pressure on Hanoi to meet certain American conditions, the chances for an agreement were the best they could ever be. There was reason for optimism. The chance to end the war was staring them in the face.

However, US presidential politics entered when it should not have. A nation united was the requirement of the time, but that was not to be. In 1968, with LBJ having stated his intention not to run for re-election, the presidential election was between on the Republican side, former vice-president under Eisenhower, Richard Nixon; on the Democratic side, the current vice-president under LBJ, Hubert H. Humphrey; and third-party candidate, former Alabama Governor George C. Wallace.

As the election neared its conclusion, Nixon saw his once formidable lead in the polls shrinking as talks of the Peace Accord were giving Humphrey a late boost in the polls, setting the stage for a closer than expected election. Nixon felt he had to do something to ensure an election victory, so his campaign devised a strategy to undermine the peace talks so that Humphrey would lose his boost and Nixon would win. Nixon's priority was winning the election before anything else – and that included the looming peace agreement. The strategy centered around unduly influencing South Vietnamese President Nguyen Van Thieu to stall the peace talks. If the peace talks stalled or failed, candidate Nixon could portray the Johnson administration's attempt at peace as a democratic failure and, thereby diminishing Humphrey, and all but guaranteeing a win in the election. This strategy was uncovered many years later and became known as the Chennault Affair. Anna Chennault was a Nixon fundraiser with access to the higher echelons in the South Vietnam government, including President Thieu himself, and she was assigned to influence Thieu to stall the talks. Working behind LBJ's back, the strategy worked, as President Thieu withdrew from the peace talks.

On November 5, 1968, Richard Nixon won the election over Hubert Humphrey and George Wallace. Nixon garnered 301 Electoral College votes to 191 for Humphrey and 46 for Wallace.Nixon also won the popular vote with 31,710,470 votes to Humphrey's 30,898,055 and Wallace's total of 9,906,473.

Nixon's actions of undermining the peace process by conspiring with a foreign government to influence United States policy could have been considered treasonous.Nixon denied all such accusations. And at the time, there was no definitive proof. Nixon had won the election and America was left to deal with the consequences — a lost opportunity for peace, a war that would last until 1975, and an untold number of casualties of war that could have been prevented. All to ensure his election.

President Lyndon B. Johnson was disgusted and very angry,

"It's despicable. ... We could stop the killing out there," Johnson insisted. "But they've got this ... new formula put in there—namely, wait on Nixon. And they're killing four or five hundred every day waiting on Nixon."

The accusations of Nixon's meddling in the peace process grew but were never fully proven until the Nixon Library released the meticulous notes of then chief-of-staff H. R. Haldeman.

The choice of Richard M. Nixon to be president proved to be a choice for the candidate that caused the most harm, not the "least harm" as Tom had hoped.

It would be five years and countless lives later, when the 27 January 27 1973 Peace Accord essentially called for an end to US involvement in Vietnam. President Nixon hailed it as "an agreement to end the war and bring peace with honor in Vietnam and Southeast Asia." These talks proved to be unsuccessful as the agreement was consistently broken by both sides. The war would only end when North Vietnamese forces overtook South Vietnam with a massive offensive in May 1975.

Day 410, 22 November 1968 – "Sure hate to get zapped this late in the game."

A letter to good friend Bill Utley..."*Getting shot down last October (29th) didn't help my nerves much either!*"

22 November 1968

Dear Bill ——-

Received your letter this afternoon along with my port call orders — I'll be saying my final farewell to Vietnam on 5 December (so close and yet so damn far away). Now all I've got to do is talk the "Old Man" into letting me quit flying combat missions within the next four or five days. Sure hate to get zapped this late in the game! Getting shot down last October (29th) didn't help my nerves much either! (my parents still don't know 'bout that either).

Glad to hear you'll be home while I am there – we'll have to have at least one out and out bullshit and drinking session — you, John, and me — ok?

The LRRP idea is a pretty good concept, especially in a war like this one, but it certainly isn't very conducive to long life — I remember too damn many times when we have had to try and save LRRP patrols in some of the most God-awful places you could imagine, and most of the times they took 100% casualties, 50 to 70% mortal.. If it's what you want, go right ahead — personally, I'll stick to helicopter gun-ships!!!

Hopefully, you may be going to my wedding sometime around Christmas, probably sometime in between Xmas & New Year's, but that, like a lot of things, remains to be seen until after I return. A whole hell of a lot can happen in 14 months, so Veda and I want to be together for a while before making any plans for the future. Who knows, we may not know each other any more!

I've got to run — take care and I'll see you Christmas ~~~~

LRRP (pronounced "lurp") was a long-range reconnaissance patrol, made up of a small, well-armed reconnaissance team that patrolled deep in enemy-held territory.

Day 412, 24 November 1968 – "I pity the first person who says something about GIs that I don't like."

Many GIs returning from Vietnam were not getting a warm welcome at this time, and soldiers in the field were hearing about it. Many were scorned, spat upon and mocked, a great disservice to these men and women who had proudly served their country.

This war was not only a tragedy of sadness, but it was also an ungrateful war with little reward and great disregard for the sacrifice of many.

24 November 1968

Dear Mom & Dad ——-

Just got back from a night scramble mission – one forward fire base was getting hit —- sure is nice how things have cooled off since the bombing halt — personally, I'm beginning to think we ought to literally sink this whole darn country and be done with it — I'm just plain fed up with getting shot at time and time again and having my hands tied with a lot of red tape 'caused by a bunch of pussy-footing politicians sitting back there in the safety & comfort of their air-conditioned offices. I pity the first person I meet back there who says something about G.I.s over here that I don't like —- I'm liable to lose my temper and cause a riot or something.

I received my orders for a port call a while ago — my freedom bird will be departing from Cam Ranh Bay on Dec. 5th at 9:30 PM — that means we should touch down at McCord AFB, Washington at the same time around 4;30 PM on the 5th of Dec. It'll be about an 18 hour flight or so, and with the international date line in between, I'll be getting there before I leave —- now, have I got you completely confused —- I hope so cause i'm sure gonna be!

Got to run —- take care and may God bless ————————-

Love,

Jim

P.S. see you soon ...!!!

Day 423, 5 December 1968 – Freedom Bird

"Freedom Bird" by T. Pueschel, December 1968

Tom survived 1968; his days in Vietnam were over. His "Freedom Bird" would depart Cam Ranh Bay on 5th of December at 9:30 PM. He would touch down on American soil — at

McCord AFB, Washington, some 18 hours later, at 4:30 PM PST on the 5th of December.

There was a great sense of joy as he boarded his freedom bird and headed home. There were also worries of his uncertain future. Thoughts of home were what got him through the tough times. It was what he thought about all the time being there. But Tom had changed and maybe others had changed back home and he did not know what to expect when he got there.

Soon he would touch American soil. But America wouldn't touch him back. America was too much involved in its own conflict to worry about a soldier coming home from war — war that America sent him into in the first place.

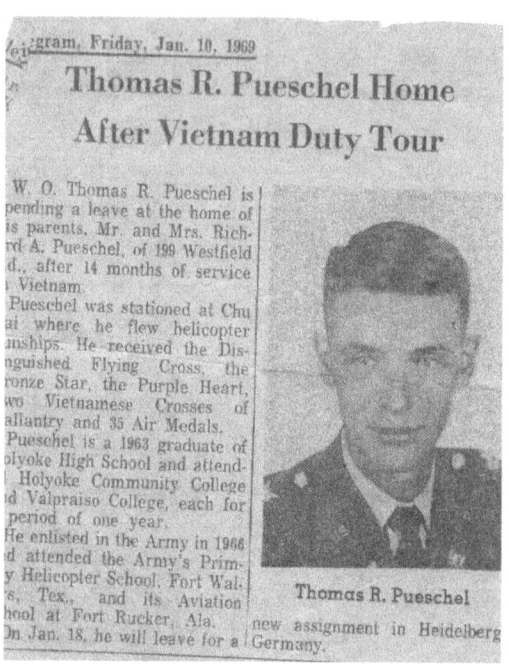

Returning Home - Holyoke Transcript newspaper - 10 Jan 1968

Sadly, US involvement in the war would last another 1,575 days past Tom's departure on Day 423 of his tour.U.S. involvement officially ended on March 29, 1973, following the January 27, 1973 peace accord. Within the sixty days following the accord, all US forces were withdrawn, all US bases dismantled, and all enemy POWs released.Over 7,000 Americans remained in South Vietnam in supporting roles.

With the US withdrawal, the "postwar war" continued for the ARVN. The South Vietnamese government remained in power for two more years after the accord. In March of 1975 the NVA began a major offensive in the central highlands and on April

30, 1975, NVA tanks rolled through Saigon to the gate of the Presidential Palace in Saigon, without resistance, effectively ending the war.Chaos ensued as the remaining Americans and many South Vietnamese escaped in a series of airlifts, sealifts, and boats. On July 2, 1976, the country was officially renamed the Socialist Republic of Vietnam with its capital in Hanoi. Saigon was now Ho Chi Minh City. Thirty years of fighting and war were officially over.

It is estimated that 58,220 US military died in the Vietnam War (per DCAS) with another 153,000 wounded in action, and untold numbers suffering PTSD and psychological injuries.

In 1995 Vietnam released its official estimate of the number of people killed during the Vietnam War: as many as 2,000,000 civilians on both sides and some 1,100,000 North Vietnamese and Viet Cong fighters. The U.S. military has estimated that between 200,000 and 250,000 South Vietnamese soldiers died. (Various internet sources.)

Postscript Vietnam

The war in Vietnam for CW2 Thomas R. Pueschel ended on 5 December 1968. From the day he stepped onto the USNS Walker on 10 October 1967, through to the end of his extended tour, Tom served 423 days, flew over 900 combat assault missions, and saw more than his share of fire and smoke and cannons and bullets and rockets.

After enduring the 18-day trip on the USNS General Walker, Tom and his unit navigated the ever-perilous Highway 19 from Qui Nhon to Pleiku. He served in the hot spots of Pleiku and Chu Lai, and he survived the bloody battles of Tam Ky and Hill

251

875, Hoi An, the battle of Dak To, multiple battles in Quang Tin province, the Tet offensive, Quang Nam, the battles of Ngok Tavak and the ratfuck bugout of Kham Duc, and countless sorties over "neutral" Cambodia and Laos. He put his life out there day after day after day. He had tempted fate and his "Invincible" moniker was jeopardized when he was shot down at Quang Ngai.

And all through the horrors of the battlefield, he fought the internal battles of his soul — honoring life and taking a life, all in the same name of duty and commitment. He earned a Purple Heart at the battle of Tam Ky, was awarded an array of medals including the Bronze Star, two Distinguished Flying Crosses, two Republic of Vietnam Cross of Gallantry medals, thirty-five Air Medals, and various others. His unit was awarded a Meritorious Unit Citation and a Presidential Unit Citation signed by the President Nixon. In most terms and definitions, he was a true combat hero, a true American hero.

But now it was time for him to come home. His family was overjoyed! But coming home was not easy. He thought maybe he lost his girl. He'd have to go see her right away. They'd have to work it out. He knew he had lost his youth. He could see it in his face, and he could feel it in his soul. He was uncertain about a lot of things. He would be barely home long enough to say 'Hello' and then it was off to Germany.

There were no big greetings awaiting veterans coming home from this war, no parades or celebrations. Protesters mis-placed their grievances about the war on the military, and on the very men and women who had done nothing wrong except to fulfill their duty, so they didn't have to. The uniform itself was dishonored so much that there was hesitation to wear it in public. Medals and acts of valor were dismissed by a public so angry with the war that they would take it out on anyone or anything associated with it.

Tom walked away but not without consequence. He left part of his soul over there. Tom would live with the scars of Vietnam his entire life. These were scars that did not go away, that did not sunset into the skin, but lingered on and arose from time to time.

"And once the storm is over, you won't remember how you made it through, how you managed to survive. You won't even be sure whether the storm is really over. But one thing is certain. When you come out of the storm, you won't be the same person who walked in. That's what this storm's all about."—Haruki Murakami (Japanese author)

Veda

Once stateside, Tom took a side trip to Indiana to visit Veda before returning to his hometown, Holyoke, Massachusetts. Veda and Tom agreed to put the marriage on hold, as Tom prepared to go to Germany. In the end, they would never get married and finally went their own ways in the months following his deployment to Germany. Tom became a confirmed bachelor for a good four years following his time in the war and in Germany.

Family

It would take until 1973 for Tom to even think of marriage again, when he met the love of his life, Gloria Lafond, a beautiful lady and a wonderful person. Tom met Gloria on a blind date, arranged by two of Gloria's soon-to-be sisters-in-law, Bonnie Pueschel and Kathy Lafond. They were married at First Lutheran Church on July 21, 1973. Later they would be married again at the Blessed Sacrament Church in Holyoke, because the Catholic Church would not acknowledge their earlier marriage in a Lutheran Church. Gloria went on to teach at the Blessed Sacrament School for over forty years, where she was one of the most highly revered teachers in the school. Tom flew for a few years after Vietnam but health derided the life-long dream. He pursued many of his other interests, always mixing in his love for art and music.

Tom and Gloria would have two fine sons, Michael and Joshua and four glorious grandchildren—Aiden, Kenzie, August, and Sheppard.

Tom didn't talk about the war much when he got home, at least in the beginning. He just went on with his life. As time went on, he opened up more and more about his time in the military. But you knew he never told you everything. Some scars are best buried. Some stories are best unsaid. Tommy Pueschel was a son, a brother, a husband, a father, a grandfather, a friend and much more. He was a proud man and a good man, a very good man. He was once a soldier, and he would always be a soldier. He was honorably discharged from the Army on 29 May 1977.

Tom and Gloria – circa 1974–1975

* * *

There's a sign on a little patch of highway in Tom's hometown of Holyoke, Massachusetts that commemorates his service and award of the Purple Heart. It's on Lincoln Street on route 202, near McNulty Park by an overlook to the Connecticut River. It is part of the Purple Heart Trail in Massachusetts.

Thank you for your service, Thomas R. Pueschel.

One of Tom's favorite pictures...

"up there singing love songs to the sky..."

Thomas Richard Pueschel

b. 3 May 1945, Holyoke, MA d. 31 January 2019

Shining star, where are you? Your light faded out much too soon.

Vietnam to Germany

Following his tour in Vietnam, Tom was deployed to Heidelberg, Germany where he would serve from 24 January 1969 through 19 December 1969. The change was great and sudden, with hardly a moment to breathe in between. Going from flying over the jungles of Vietnam to flying over the streets of Germany was a transition that he appeared to do with ease. But truth be told, it would take him some time to overcome his sense of loss and find some focus moving forward. It would be a struggle that he would have to deal with for the rest of his life. Nothing would ever compare with the mode of war.Nothing would ever erase its memories.

The following are some excerpts from the letters he wrote home during his time in Germany.

24 December 1968 – Getting squared away in Germany

A welcome-to-the-unit letter to Tom as he began his stay In Germany, where he was assigned to the 207th Aviation Company:

207th AVIATION COMPANY
APO 09102

24 December, 1968

CW2 Thomas R. Pueschel
119 Westfield Road
Holyoke, Mass. 01040

Dear Mr. Pueschel:

As of now I am the only bachelor in the unit. You won't have any problem
getting settled at all. I'll take care of getting your quarters for you.
I live in the BOQ, and it is more than adequat. The BOQ is two rooms,
one living room, one bedroom, with a bathroom and shower. The Officer's
Club is across the street from the BOQ, which is quite a convenience.
I just called the BOQ office and they told me that I won't be able to
sign for your quarters until the 10th of Jan.

Upon your arrival here I will take you around and get you all squared away.
There won't be any problems there. If you have a car I suggest that you
bring it with you. It is almost impossible to get around here without
one. If you don't have a car there are always ones for sale here by
people who are leaving.

The Warrant officer and commisioned officer relationship couldn't be better.
You'll like your situation here. At the present time we have 4 W2's (you'll
make 5), 1 W3, 3 W4's, 3 Cpt's, 3Maj's, and 2 Ltc's. So we outnumber the
commisions. We all share the work load and nobody is over-worked. We
work in a very relaxed atmosphere, with only a minimum of rank consciousness.
It's like they taught you in school; all Warrants are called by their first
names as are lieutenants, Captains are called Captain, and field grade is
called Sir.

Well that's all for now, if you think of anything else feel free to call
on me.

Sincerely,

CW2 McConnell Coakwell

24 January 1969 – "Heidelberg is pretty nice."

*"Just a few lines to let you know that I have arrived in Germany
in one piece and am fast becoming a part of things around here. I
didn't get out of Fort Dix until the 29th...You don't have to worry
about sending my flight suits 'cause in my unit over here they fly
in dress greens because we're always flying generals and such...
Heidelberg is pretty nice (especially the girls). I haven't much time
to look around, but I got a pretty good look at it from the air —>*

259

they sent a helicopter up to Frankfurt to get me when they found out I was there."

27 January 1969 – "All washed up for good in the end."

"I received your letter a couple of days ago along with a bunch of other mail from people I know — sure feels good to get mail so soon, but still nothing from Veda – I have a feeling that we are going to be all washed up for good in the end."

13 February 1969 – "To take a train in Germany."

Tom was at the Gablingen - Kaserne Army Airfield for orientation and training.

"At the moment, I am in a German hotel here in Augsburg called the :Alpenhof" where I am staying while I attend the two days of classes for us new guys at the Gablingen - Kaserne Army airfield, which is located just outside Augsburg. It has been snowing like crazy all week and doesn't show any signs of letting up either, which is why we came down here on a train instead of driving.To take a train in Germany is an experience — it's a good thing I can speak a little German or I and the two guys I came down with would never have made it! They don't speak a word and understand less! The trains here are unbelievable — they are <u>on time,</u> for one thing, and they don't stop in any one place for very long — about four minutes, if you're lucky.Also, we ate lunch on board, °and they really heaped the plates high — for only DM 6.00 (DM = Deutsche Mark) I had meat, mashed potatoes, and sauerkraut plus coffee and cake, and that's pretty good for only what amounts to $1.50 (4 DM = $1.00 US) especially on a train!"

15 February 1969 – "Snowing like crazy."

"Grüsse aus Heidelberg! I have just returned from the orientation

course in Augsburg at Gablingen-Kaserne airfield. It wasn't too bad, but the weather could have been a whole lot better.It has been snowing like crazy here in Germany for at least a week, and it is getting to be a colossal pain in the neck. That VW of mine just wasn't made to go plowing through about a foot and a half of that cold white stuff, and I'm not about to spend the money for a set of snow tires which probably would not too much anyway. So, I guess I'll just have to be content to be sliding around for a while until the snow is all gone —- that's all right though, for I've gone sliding around before and will again, so why fight city hall? .... This is the last week-end of Fasching, somewhat of a damper on the festivities, but the parties will go none the less."

Note: Fasching (also known as Karneval) is **a time of festivity and merry making** - a time to break the rules, poke fun at those who make them and then to make your own new rules. In Germany, particularly in the Rhineland area, the tradition can be traced to medieval times where many countries existed under harsh rules. (Source: internet search)

13 March 1969 – "Your son's a pilot."

"I'm sort of glad I didn't bring my Corvair over here — I'm going to need a car when I get back and will probably have enough bills to worry about without car payments added in. I have written to a couple of schools — Embry-Riddle Aeronautical Institute for one, and am planning on going back to school — full-time, if I can, and what with tuition, room & board, and all the other extraneous expenses connected with college, I'll probably end up in hock up to my ears for a couple of years. Guess I'm going to have to find some rich girl and marry her for the money! All in all, it really shouldn't be too bad — as a bachelor, I can get $130.00 per month form the

Veterans Administration plus up to 90% of my tuition as long as it is flight training, which I want and can get at Embry-Riddle in Florida. If I go there, I can get a Bachelor of Science degree in Aeronautical Science and fixed-wing, multi-engine instrument flight training in aircraft ranging from a single-engine light plane (Piper Cub) on up to a Boeing 707, and will be qualified for a commercial rating. They also have job placement there and will get you a job with one of the airlines upon graduation, which would suit me just fine. Some, but not all of my college credits will be transferable and my Army flight school and helicopter flight time will all count.We shall see, though — even with V.A., it's still going to cost a bunch and I imagine I'll have to find a job somewhere — perhaps flying helicopters, if I can pass that F.A.A. exam for my commercial helicopter ticket! So you see — your son's a pilot and will remain so come hell or high water — I don't think I'd be happy doing anything else!

....Tell Ken Happy Birthday and on wine, women, and song — (he's not getting any younger!). I still can't picture him with a pipe though — are you sure it's not a bubble pipe???"

5 April 1969 – "Great feeling to be a teacher."

"I'm glad that Dad liked the bier steins... I was wondering when they would get there...I have been doing quite a bit of oil painting lately, and have also been holding sort of informal art classes with some of the wives of guys in my unit who are sort of trying their hand at it. Somehow or other, they found out I can draw a little, and they have been asking me for advice, which I am only too happy to give...besides, I usually end up getting a free, home-cooked dinner in the process, so it seems to be well worth my while...some of them are darn good at oil painting, too, but they don't know all the tricks and short-cuts that I have been able to pick up over the

years which make some things a whole lot easier, and then they seem very surprised at how simple and easy it all can turn out to be ... anyway, it's fun and I seem to be learning just as much as they are, only in a different respect.It must be a great feeling to be a teacher sometimes.

Right now I've got three paintings of my own that are hanging in my rooms, and I have already sold two... I imagine if I keep on at this rate, I will be up to my neck in them before long, so don't be surprised if some day you get an oil painting or two in the mail with my name on it..."

20 April 1969 – On marriage...

"After all, marriage is an institution, love is a state of mind, and my state of mind refuses to let me be institutionalized."

15 May 1969 – "Land of the miniskirt."

Roommates in Germany were matchmaking.

"You know, I kind of like being a free and fun-loving bachelor... maybe even too much to ever spoil it all by getting married...right now I am enjoying my freedom very much, and with the tourist season coming up, it should be even more enjoyable and interesting with even more than already abundant number of pretty girls walking around Heidleberg....

I'm planning on going to England around the 20th of next month...they call London the "Land of the Miniskirt" so it should be very interesting to say the least"

5 June 1969 – Kid Brothers

Tom's brothers were trying to figure out their own lives:

"You can tell that kid brother of mine that if he quits school and goes into the service, I'll kick his butt from here halfway around

the world, change feet, and kick him the rest of the way!!!"

5 June 1969 – "I know what he's in for."

Tom's boyhood friend, Billy Utley was heading to Vietnam:

"Billy's going to the land of flaming rice paddy in August, huh? I don't envy him a bit, especially since he's going to be on the ground, but then, us pilots never did relish being on the ground, even though we were more or less sitting ducks up there with nothing to hide behind when the shooting started. I wish him a whole bunch of luck...I know what he's in for and he will too, before long."

Note: Bill Utley was commissioned as a 2nd Lieutenant (2LT) in the Infantry in June 1968, having been part of the ROTC program at Syracuse University. Bill would go to Vietnam in August 1969 as a company platoon leader, company executive officer, and Battalion S-3 Air (Air ops). He served there with Charlie, Echo (Heavy Weapons), and Headquarters Company, 1st Battalion, 501st Infantry Regiment, 101st Airborne Division (Airmobile). At about his 10-month mark, he was in a Huey that got shot down while out delivering replacement signal operating instructions to teams in the field. He suffered heavy shrapnel wounds and was evacuated out of Vietnam through Japan and then back home. He recovered from his injuries and would later serve with the Secret Service.

11 June 1969 – Sports Cars and Marriage

"I guess you must have heard about the sports car I'm getting by now... can't wait til it gets here. It is something I always wanted, but never got around to getting and besides, it is just the right kind of car for a fun-loving and SINGLE bachelor pilot like me to have

to ride around in when I'm not up there singing love songs to the sky...

You can tell Dad that there is not too much to worry about me coming home married... that's about the furthest thing from my mind right now, money or no money! If I ever do get married, I think it will be at least a couple of years from now, if not more, 'cause I'm not even ready to even start thinking of it, much less doing it! ..."

11 June 1969 – "For once in my life."

Tom talking up his new red sports car! Triumph!

"...I kind of like the idea of for once in my life having a car that is not what you might call practical... What I mean is that for once I did not buy a car for its gas mileage or low cost or room or anything, but because it was what I've wanted for a long time, even if its gas mileage is pretty good and it did not really cost me that much...as for the room, well...it doesn't have a whole lot, but how much room does a bachelor need, especially when there might be a girl here or there with whom he may want to get better acquainted."

21 July 1969 – "Men on the moon."

The die-hards stayed up all night watching them land on the moon!

"So, what do you think of the men on the moon??? I think it is utterly fantastic and I'd have given my right arm to have been up there with them...as it was, though, I and a few other diehards stayed up all night and watched them on German TV. Back there in the US, you people had it easy because it was at a reasonable time of day... over here, it wasn't until four AM when they finally landed. That was alright, though, 'cause they set up a TV in the Officer's Club and served breakfast from 3 until 9 AM...I only had

breakfast three times this morning, but then I don't really have to worry about my weight, do I?"

21 July 1969 – "Fixing toys and playing big brother."

"I've gotten involved with a little orphanage where I spend quite a bit of time fixing toys and sort of playing big brother to a bunch of little kids who plain haven't got anyone else in the world who gives a damn. I enjoy going up there very much, and it has gotten so that if something comes up where I can't make it that particular week, the Sisters who run the place have a bunch of very disappointed kids on their hands, and I get twice as big a welcome the next time I come."

7 August 1969 – "I LOVE it now!!"

"I got my Triumph about a week ago, and though, I liked it when I ordered it, I LOVE it now!!!"

7 August 1969 – "Life."

"Yes, I guess Larry has changed quite a bit since he went to U of M...he's got to pick his own way, though...no one can help him 'cause it's all part of growing up...some things you just have to do on your own...I sort of found my own way up to the present time, and sometimes I wonder if I've really come all that far... also, I sometimes wonder if perhaps I grew up too fast and missed something somewhere along the line...even so, for a guy who is only twenty-four years old, I have certainly been to a lot of different places and done a lot of very different things, and I think that I have come to love being alive that much more...I have finally found that life is something to be thoroughly enjoyed from the day you are born to your last mortal breath, and I intend to do just that!"

13 August 1969 – "Goes like a bat out of hades."

"Enclosed is a snapshot of my new Triumph...It's red with black interior and it goes like a bat out of hades!!! I love it, even if my present girlfriend does have a little trouble getting in and out of it with a skirt on!"

28 August 1969 – "If a next time ever comes into being."

"I'm happy to hear that Veda finally sent you that scrapbook... She and I have drifted pretty far apart...we're not even writing to each other anymore...Guess that was one romance that just wasn't meant to be, even if it still hurts a little. That's ok, though...it'll just make me that much more cautious the next time, if a next time ever comes into being"

18 September 1969 – "Sprayed...with jet fuel."

"Last Friday, some dumb idiot backed into my brand-new Triumph with a truck in the PX parking lot... as if this weren't enough, ...while they were refueling my helicopter up by Kastle, I was sprayed from head to toe with JP-4 (jet fuel), also getting a bunch in my eyes.Luckily, I happened to have a flight surgeon on board at the time, and there was A German first aid station nearby where they washed out my eyes and put ointment in them to neutralize the acids in the fuel before it did any damage to my eyes... otherwise, I probably would have been in the market for a seeing eye dog and a white cane not long thereafter... if you think that is enough, hold on...last Saturday night, ...my left lung collapsed, giving me all the symptoms of a heart attack. .... they had to cut a hole in my chest and insert a tube to suck out the excess air around the outside of my lung so as to alleviate the pressure and allow my lung to inflate again.... all over now... bed rest and tender loving care from all my girlfriends ... I'll be off flight status for quite

a while and that's what hurts the most, but at least I'll be able to fly again in another two to three weeks .... If it had grounded me permanently, I think I would have died from a broken heart."

24 October 1969 – "The annual Aviation Ball...a gala affair."

"They have been keeping me pretty busy with a lot of miscellaneous administrative paperwork and also doing a lot of preparations for the annual Aviation Ball, which will be coming up on the 14th of next month — Bobbi, the nurse I'm dating, is looking forward to it quite a lot, but as for me, I'm looking forward ot it with apprehension.I always feel like a doorman or something when I have to wear my dress blues. Anyway, since my unit is sponsoring the whole mess this year, I and just about everyone else in the 207th have our hands full with the preparations, and since there will be somewhere in the neighborhood of eight Generals attending, it will be what you might call a gala affair — I just hope I live through it!!!"

28 October 1969 – Out three months early, on 19 December!!!

*"When I went into work yesterday morning, I found quite a surprise waiting for me — it seems that Uncle Sam is going to let me out of the Army almost three months early, on 19 **December**!!! That means I've only got about fifty-two more days left before I shed my uniform and trade it in for civilian clothes, and I can't say that I'm heartbroken at that prospect! Even so, I have sort of mixed feelings..."*

6 November 1969 – "All red tape in getting out of the army."

*"As it stands at the present time, I will be leaving Europe, but I imagine that it will be prior to my discharge date of 19 **December** by at least two or three days... I guess I will probably have to remain*

at Fort Dix, for a couple days so as to wade through all the red tape involved in getting out of the army..."

19 December 1969 – Out of the Army Now

I'm out of the Army, now. I'm out of the Army, now! Back behind a plow!!

Tom really believed this...